This book is a

Gift

From

....

To

....

Date

....

May God bless you through this book

PRAYERS FOR A SUCCESSFUL CAREER

PRAYERS FOR A SUCCESSFUL CAREER

PRAYER M. MADUEKE

PRAYER PUBLICATIONS
1 Babatunde close, Off Olaitan Street,
Surulere, Lagos, Nigeria
+234 803 353 0599

PRAYERS FOR A SUCCESSFUL CAREER

PRAYER M. MADUEKE

ISBN: 9781492917076

Prayer Publications

Unless otherwise indicated, all Scripture quotations are taken from the King James Version of the Bible, and used by permission. All emphasis within quotations is the author's additions.

First Edition, 2013

For further information of permission

1 Babatunde close, off Olaitan Street, Surulere, Lagos, Nigeria
+234 803 353 0599
Email: pastor@prayermadueke.com,
Website: www.prayermadueke.com

Table of Contents

COMPREHENSIVE PRAYER LIST

DEDICATION

This book is dedicated to individuals and families, who are sincerely trusting God for blessing and healing according to His Word.

"Then they cried unto the LORD in their trouble, and he saveth them out of their distresses. [20]He sent his word, and healed them, and delivered them from their destructions" (Psalms 107:19-20).

OWNERS OF EVIL LOAD

CHAPTER OVERVIEW

- *What is an evil load?*
- *Instances of evil load*
- *How to return evil loads to their owners*
- *Destined to overcome*
- *Spiritual warfare*
- *Provision, promise and victory*
- *Divine provision*
- *God promise, power and victory*
- *General prayers*

"[7]So went Satan forth from the presence of the LORD, and smote Job with sore boils from the sole of his foot unto his crown" (Job 2:7).

This passage, and several other passages, of the Scriptures have continued to confound many Christians, including bible scholars. How could Satan appear in the presence of the LORD, and even gained an audience from God? How could God have allowed that? Well, simply, only God knows. But one truth that played out in the above scripture is that Satan and all his demons are the chief sources of all sicknesses, afflictions and attacks on earth. They intend no good for any man. Although other causes of disasters can be argued, but Satan is at the helm of all evil and wickedness. Sin is his most successful weapon.

> *"[44]Ye are of your father the devil, and the lusts of your father ye will do. He was a murderer from the beginning, and abode not in the truth, because there is no truth in him. When he speaketh a lie, he speaketh of his own: for he is a liar, and the father of it"* (John 8:44).

> *"[14]Afterward Jesus findeth him in the temple, and said unto him, Behold, thou art made whole: sin no more, lest a worse thing come unto thee"* (John 5:14).

God's plan and will for any man has never been of evil, but good. That's how we know that the frustration, confusion and depression most people go through are not from God, but from Satan, including all spiritual and physical problems. Since God expelled him from heaven, he hasn't relented but consistently attacked God's universe and God's people. He is the originator of all evil works, having recruited millions of humans into his army of evildoers. The Scriptures also called him the accuser of the brethren, adversary, ruler of darkness, sinner and murderer of good things and people on earth.

"[10]And I heard a loud voice saying in heaven, Now is come salvation, and strength, and the kingdom of our God, and the power of his Christ: for the accuser of our brethren is cast down, which accused them before our God day and night" (Revelation 12:10).

> *"[8]Be sober, be vigilant; because your adversary the devil, as a roaring lion, walked about, seeking whom he may devour"* (1 Peter 5:8).
>
> *"[12]For we wrestle not against flesh and blood, but against principalities, against powers, against the rulers of the darkness of this world, against spiritual wickedness in high places"* (Ephesians 6:12).
>
> *"[8]The wind bloweth where it listeth, and thou hearest the sound thereof, but canst not tell whence it cometh, and whither it goeth: so is every one that is born of the Spirit"* (John 3:8).

Lucifer, as his name also was, is the father of all lies and evil worker. He can enter into any person's life through sin, idolatry, evil inheritance, consultation with familiar spirits, occultism, palm reading, hypnotism, witchcraft, etc. Equally, failure to resist him can prove to be detrimental.

> *"[14]But the Spirit of the LORD departed from Saul, and an evil spirit from the LORD troubled him. [15]And Saul's servants said unto him, Behold now, an evil spirit from God troubled thee"*(1 Samuel 16:14-15).
>
> *"[27]Neither give place to the devil"* (Ephesians 4:27).
>
> *"[7]Submit yourselves therefore to God. Resist the devil, and he will flee from you"* (James 4:7).

Whenever you cooperate with evil spirits or open your heart to occult practices, Satan quickly takes advantage of such opportunity to plant evil seeds in your life. And when you keep properties like charms, amulets, occult books, etc., in your house, Satan stays in your house to guard such materials.

"[25]*And it came to pass the same night, that the LORD said unto him, Take thy father's young bullock, even the second bullock of seven years old, and throw down the altar of Baal that thy father hath, and cut down the grove that is by it:* [26]*And build an altar unto the LORD thy God upon the top of this rock, in the ordered place, and take the second bullock, and offer a burnt sacrifice with the wood of the grove which thou shalt cut down*" (Judges 6:25-26).

"[8]*Beware lest any man spoil you through philosophy and vain deceit, after the tradition of men, after the rudiments of the world, and not after Christ*" (Colossians 2:8).

"[18]*And many that believed came, and confessed, and shewed their deeds.* [19]*Many of them also which used curious arts brought their books together, and burned them before all men: and they counted the price of them, and found it fifty thousand pieces of silver*" (Acts 19:18-19).

It is useless to be seeking after God when you know you have dealings with Satan. He cannot let you seek God. Unless you repent, confess and forsake your sins, and then renounce devil, burning all his properties, you cannot make any headway. But when you have confessed your sins, declare that Jesus is the Son of God and accept Him as your Savior. Your life receives transformation and you become a new person in the spirit. You cannot afford to miss this opportunity.

WHAT IS AN EVIL LOAD?

In simplest term, evil load is a generic term, which also means evil liability, which is beyond your power to pluck out of your life. Satan is the source of evil loads, and it takes the power and grace of God to throw away evil loads. However, evil loads can also be describe as -

- *Oppression; an arched device laid upon a victim to torment his life until death.*
- *A satanic restriction to achievements or limitation.*
- *Any demonic material that can bring visible or invisible problems into a person's life.*
- *A yoke that brings her victims under bondage or servitude.*
- *An instrument of agony.*
- *A plague of sickness, torment or affliction.*

It is nearly impossible to succeed when you are under the yoke of an evil load. Unless you discover the presence of any on time and do away with it through prayers, you cannot comfortably operate with success in anything you set out to achieve. This is because the purpose of evil loads is to stop your advancement, and if possible, destroy or ruin your destiny.

A perfect example of an evil load was clearly seen in the case of Samson and Delilah. Samson thought he had married a beautiful and lovely wife. But indeed, Delilah was a terrible evil load. We saw what happened. Samson was able to slaughter thousands of Philistine armies, but failing to destroy his evil load, it destroyed Samson.

What appears to be a small evil load can actually bring down a mighty man. Or influence him to take wrong and disheartening decisions. Evil loads have captured and wasted many people's lives and destinies. They have killed and buried many mighty men and women already. They have diverted so many people to reject good people and accept dangerous enemies as spouses.

Evil load can blind one's spiritual eyes; pup evil marks of hatred on such person. That's why many people experience a never-ending rejection wherever they go. When you fail to send evil loads back to their owners, they can shut your doors of success and opportunities forever. But such will not be your case in the name of Jesus.

> "[16]*They that see thee shall narrowly look upon thee, and consider thee, saying, Is this the man that made the earth to tremble, that did shake kingdoms;* [17]*That made the world as a wilderness, and destroyed the cities thereof; that opened not the house of his prisoners?"* (Isaiah 14:16-17)

> "[2]*And Pharaoh said, Who is the LORD, that I should obey his voice to let Israel go? I know not the LORD, neither will I let Israel go.* [3]*And they said, The God of the Hebrews hath met with us: let us go, we pray thee, three days' journey into the desert, and sacrifice unto the LORD our God; lest he fall upon us with pestilence, or with the sword.* [4]*And the king of Egypt said unto them, Wherefore do ye, Moses and Aaron, let the people from their works? Get you unto your burdens"*(Exodus 5:2-4).

A wise Christian would not want to live with any evil liability. Whatever that is capable of preventing you from making heaven is not worth keeping. That's why you have to do whatever that is possible to send evil loads back to senders, or at least, destroy them. Only then can you live a fulfilled life; a life that is free from evil riots, storms, failures, bad habits and struggles without success. Evil loads are capable of keeping people away from God's plan and promises. They bring disgrace, fear, indecision and curses upon people. Their mission is to kill and bury people. But when you confront evil loads through prayers, you are sure to win because God has already overcome the world in Christ Jesus for your sake. And your prosperity, life, marriage and family will remain secured in the grace of God through Christ Jesus.

> "[29]*And thou shalt grope at noonday, as the blind*

gropeth in darkness, and thou shalt not prosper in thy ways: and thou shalt be only oppressed and spoiled evermore, and no man shall save thee. [30]Thou shalt betroth a wife, and another man shall lie with her: thou shalt build a house, and thou shalt not dwell therein: thou shalt plant a vineyard, and shalt not gather the grapes thereof. [31]Thine ox shall be slain before thine eyes, and thou shalt not eat thereof: thine ass shall be violently taken away from before thy face, and shall not be restored to thee: thy sheep shall be given unto thine enemies, and thou shalt have none to rescue them. [32]Thy sons and thy daughters shall be given unto another people, and thine eyes shall look, and fail with longing for them all the daylong: and there shall be no might in thine hand. [33]The fruit of thy land, and all thy labors, shall a nation which thou knowest not eat up; and thou shalt be only oppressed and crushed always" (Deuteronomy 28:29-33).

"[36]The LORD shall bring thee, and thy king which thou shalt set over thee, unto a nation which neither thou nor thy fathers have known; and there shalt thou serve other gods, wood and stone. [37]And thou shalt become an astonishment, a proverb, and a byword, among all nations whither the LORD shall lead thee. [38]Thou shalt carry much seed out into the field, and shalt gather but little in; for the locust shall consume it. [39]Thou shalt plant vineyards, and dress them, but shalt neither drink of the wine, nor gather the grapes; for the worms shall eat them. [40]Thou shalt have olive trees throughout all thy coasts, but thou shalt not anoint thyself with the oil; for thine olive shall cast his fruit" (Deuteronomy 28:36-40).

It is good at this point to mention various types of evil loads you need to do away with at all cost in order to live a meaningful or purposeful life on earth. They include personal, generational, family, tribal, traditional, environmental, inherited and national evil loads. None of these liabilities deserves to thrive in your life.

INSTANCES OF EVIL LOAD

Many couples failed in marriage because they failed to identity evil loads, which beset their marriage. There are some liabilities that when they plague your marriage, it will surely collapse in the cause of time. These kinds instigate divorces, separation and disheartening break ups. Equally, some specifically target businesses and academics. These evil loads are the source of infertility and sicknesses. See if you can identify any of these evil loads:

- *Evil appetite and lust for sexual satisfaction*
- *Load of impossibility*
- *Load of late marriage*
- *Load of poverty*
- *Load of demotion and rejection*
- *Load of none-achievement*
- *Load of memory failure and fear*
- *Load of disfavor*
- *Load of hardship*

HOW TO RETURN EVIL LOADS TO THEIR OWNERS

Here are few steps you can take to disown and dislodge any evil load that you identify operating in your life or that of your family. First, you have to realize that it would be humanly impossible to win spiritual battle, but possible with God. So, that means you have to bring God in to relieve you of all evil liabilities as you continue to trust in His mercy.

1. You have to be born-again. This is the first major step. You cannot avoid this step. "*Jesus answered and said unto him, Verily, verily, I say unto thee, Except a man be born-again, he cannot see the kingdom of God*" (John 3:3).

2. Repent and forsake your sins truly and thoroughly. You have to make up your mind on which side you want to be. Do you want to be on God's side or remain on devil's side? When you determine you want to come to God, you have to repent and forsake your sins in order to obtain mercy from God.

   "[13]*He that covereth his sins shall not prosper: but whoso confesseth and forsaketh them shall have mercy*" (Proverbs 28:13).

   "[3]*And Samuel spake unto all the house of Israel, saying, If ye do return unto the LORD with all your hearts, then put away the strange gods and Ashtaroth from among you, and prepare your hearts unto the LORD, and serve him only: and he will deliver you out of the hand of the Philistines.* [4]*Then the children of Israel did put away Baalim and Ashtaroth, and served the LORD only*" (1 Samuel 7:3-4).

3. You must have faith in God. You must be ready to trust in God and His mercy. This means that you have to start learning what it means to walk by faith and not by sight. You have to understand that God's ways are different from what you are accustomed to. So, whether what you

are seeing makes sense to you or not, do not believe it. Trust in God's mercy and have faith.

4. Pray aggressive until you get results. As you pray, be expectant that God will do a miracle for you. And like Jesus always said, you faith will heal and deliver you from all satanic loads and liabilities.

DESTINED TO OVERCOME

Every human that is born of a woman is engaged in one form of spiritual battle or another. The forces of darkness in this world contend with the forces of light and righteousness continually. And humans are caught up in the crossfire. But only true believers experience complete victory through Christ Jesus.

At the end of his ministry, Paul declared, *"[7]I have fought a good fight, I have finished my course, I have kept the faith"* (2 Timothy 4:7). He knew all along that he was fighting a spiritual warfare. What about you? Are you aware of your battles?

Many go through spiritual battles without being born-again. How do you expect to win? Battling the devil without being born-again cannot be a good fight. You cannot win. Unfortunately, majority of the people on earth are ignorant of the ongoing spiritual conflicts. They simply relate every battle going on in their lives to physical challenges. Such people are at the losing end. Regardless of how much wealth you can coordinate to solve every problem, you cannot win. Your battles will keep coming back in many other forms.

It is a wise thing to be conscious of the fact that everything that has physical dimension also has spiritual dimension. Most people on earth are under the bondage of one sin or another. You have to recognize that there is a demon behind every kind of sin. And such demons can only be addressed successfully through spiritual means, in this case prayer. The truth is that, if you are under the oppression of an evil spirit, you cannot reign over some circumstances even as a Christian.

> *"[10]And he was teaching in one of the synagogues on the Sabbath. [11]And, behold, there was a woman, which had a spirit of infirmity eighteen years, and was bowed together, and could in no wise lift up herself. [12]And when Jesus saw her, he called her to him, and said unto her, Woman, thou art loosed from thine*

infirmity. [13]And he laid his hands on her: and immediately she was made straight, and glorified God" (Luke 13:10-13).

"[16]And ought not this woman, being a daughter of Abraham, whom Satan hath bound, lo, these eighteen years, be loosed from this bond on the Sabbath day?" (Luke 13:16).

Let's take for instance, this woman that Satan bound for eighteen years. She was a true child of God, born-again and daughter of Abraham. Yet, Satan took her hostage for eighteen years. The source of her deliverance showed up but she was ignorant of Him. Satan tormented her with evil spirit of infirmity until Jesus said it was enough.

What is that sickness or disease in your life, which Jesus cannot bring to an end? Jesus is the deliverance that you have been praying and seeking for.

"[32]And ye shall know the truth, and the truth shall make you free... [36]If the Son therefore shall make you free, ye shall be free indeed" (John 8:32, 36).

Now that you have known the truth; that Jesus Christ, the Son of God, is the Lord and Savior of your life, you must act in faith at once, in order to be free from evil bondages. It also means that it is now time to resist the devil. If you are not born-again yet, do not waste any second more. Confess that Jesus is your Lord and Savior and receive Him in your heart today.

"[3]Jesus answered and said unto him, Verily, verily, I say unto thee, Except a man be born again, he can not see the kingdom of God" (John 3:3).

"[7]Submit yourselves therefore to God. Resist the devil, and he will flee from you" (James 4:7).

SPIRITUAL WARFARE

There is always a fight to fight and only those, who are born-again and know how to use God's Word has hope to have the victory. If you still have sin reigning inside of you, you are bound to die in your bondage. That is why being born-again is a necessity if you must succeed.

> "[23]*But I see another law in my members, warring against the law of my mind, and bringing me into captivity to the law of sin which is in my members"* (Romans 7:23).

> "[12]*For we wrestle not against flesh and blood, but against principalities, against powers, against the rulers of the darkness of this world, against spiritual wickedness in high places"* (Ephesians 6:12).

The battle within is more dangerous than the battle without. Sin is more destructive than the physical problem you are going through now. Your weak character and all acquired bad habits are worse than every physical problem you are going through now. Sin empowers every problem and makes the conflict fiercer. You may need to relocate your tent from Sodom and overcome your tempting Delilah so that through Jesus, you may receive access to healing and deliverance.

> "[10]*And he was teaching in one of the synagogues on the Sabbath.* [11]*And, behold, there was a woman, which had a spirit of infirmity eighteen years, and was bowed together, and could in no wise lift up herself.* [12]*And when Jesus saw her, he called her to him, and said unto her, Woman, thou art loosed from thine infirmity.* [13]*And he laid his hands on her: and immediately she was made straight, and glorified God.* [14]*And the ruler of the synagogue answered with indignation, because that Jesus had healed on the Sabbath day, and said unto the people, There are six days in which men ought to work: in them therefore come and be healed, and not on the Sabbath day.* [15]*The Lord then answered him, and said, Thou hypocrite,*

doth not each one of you on the Sabbath loose his ox or his ass from the stall, and lead him away to watering? [16]And ought not this woman, being a daughter of Abraham, whom Satan hath bound, lo, these eighteen years, be loosed from this bond on the Sabbath day?"(Luke 13:10-16)

It is of no use praying for physical healing, deliverance and prosperity if you are not ready to fight sin first.

"[6]Jesus saith unto him, I am the way, the truth, and the life: no man cometh unto the Father, but by me" (John 14:6).

Jesus said unto him, *"[13]He that covereth his sins shall not prosper: but whoso confesseth and forsaketh them shall have mercy"* (Proverbs 28:13).

The battle of life is sweet with assurance of victory if you are ready to repent, confess and forsake all your sins. You cannot stay outside your Father, Savior and in far country and fight your life's battle successfully. You need to come back to your source, creator and your God.

"[17]And when he came to himself, he said, How many hired servants of my father's have bread enough and to spare, and I perish with hunger! [18]I will arise and go to my father, and will say unto him, Father, I have sinned against heaven, and before thee, [19]And am no more worthy to be called thy son: make me as one of thy hired servants. [20]And he arose, and came to his father. But when he was yet a great way off, his father saw him, and had compassion, and ran, and fell on his neck, and kissed him. [21]And the son said unto him, Father, I have sinned against heaven, and in thy sight, and am no more worthy to be called thy son. [22]But the father said to his servants, Bring forth the best robe, and put it on him; and put a ring on his hand, and shoes on his feet: [23]And bring hither the fatted calf, and kill it; and let us eat, and be merry: [24]For this my son was dead, and is alive again; he was lost, and is found. And they began to be merry" (Luke 15:17-24).

As a born again Christian, you can be sure of victory when you start praying. No matter how strong you are, how wealthy you are and how wise you are, you cannot win the battles of life without your Savior. Spiritual battles cannot be fought with human techniques. Being strong in occultism, witchcrafts and evil cannot give you true and lasting victory. You have to be strong in the Lord. You can only receive true answers to your prayers and full deliverance by fighting with God's amour.

> "[10]*Finally, my brethren, be strong in the Lord, and in the power of his might.* [11]*Put on the whole armor of God that ye may be able to stand against the wiles of the devil.* [12]*For we wrestle not against flesh and blood, but against principalities, against powers, against the rulers of the darkness of this world, against spiritual wickedness in high places*" (Ephesians 6:10-12).

Without the grace of God and the power of the Spirit of God, any of us will be as weak as the fallen giants. Experience has shown that minor problems can defeat those who lean on their human ability to fight the devil. No matter your experience, ability and maturity, if you don't lean on God and start praying, this problem will overcome you.

> "[28]*Hast thou not known? Hast thou not heard, that the everlasting God, the LORD, the Creator of the ends of the earth, fainteth not, neither is weary? there is no searching of his understanding.* [29]*He giveth power to the faint; and to them that have no might he increaseth strength.* [30]*Even the youths shall faint and be weary, and the young men shall utterly fall:* [31]*But they that wait upon the LORD shall renew their strength; they shall mount up with wings as eagles; they shall run, and not be weary; and they shall walk, and not faint*" (Isaiah 40:28-31).

If you need to fast, don't delay, if you need to pray for many nights, wake up to pray until your deliverance comes true. Let your greatest concern be to win and receive full deliverance. People, who overcome, are known for their resilience in prayer, vigilance, faith and resistance until the end. As a true child of God, you are destined to overcome every problem including the present ones in the name of Jesus.

PROVISION, PROMISE AND VICTORY

God has made adequate provision and has given precious promises by which every believer can receive and enjoy the best of life on earth. Christ suffered and died for this purpose. You can obtain every good thing promised by God by recognizing the need in your life.

> "[9]*And Jabez was more honorable than his brethren: and his mother called his name Jabez, saying, Because I bare him with sorrow.* [10]*And Jabez called on the God of Israel, saying, Oh that thou wouldest bless me indeed, and enlarge my coast, and that thine hand might be with me, and that thou wouldest keep me from evil, that it may not grieve me! And God granted him that which he requested*" (1 Chronicles 4:9-10).

> "[11]*For the LORD God is a sun and shield: the LORD will give grace and glory: no good thing will he withhold from them that walk uprightly*" (Psalms 84:11).

Jabez recognized the need for change, blessing and deliverance from all evil in his life. He became thirsty for change. The thirst and hunger led him into action. He wholeheartedly consecrated his life to God, holding back nothing and God never disappointed him.

> "[22]*And all things, whatsoever ye shall ask in prayer, believing, ye shall receive*" (Matthew 21:22).

> "[3]*According as his divine power hath given unto us all things that pertain unto life and godliness, through the knowledge of him that hath called us to glory and virtue:* [4]*Whereby are given unto us exceeding great and precious promises: that by these ye might be partakers of the divine nature, having escaped the corruption that is in the world through lust*" (2 Peter 1:3-4).

If you have faith in God's promise, and pray, claim his promises, He will not say no. There are many great and precious promises waiting for you to be claimed in this program. It is not enough for you to know what God has promised you through his word. You have to fight every power that will try to stop you from enjoying them. No matter how long it takes you have to persist until all the oppressors' bows. Through consistent Christian life, prayer and even fasting, you must insist until you receive and enjoy all that Christ has provided for you through God's promise.

> "[6]*Be careful for nothing; but in every thing by prayer and supplication with thanksgiving let your requests be made known unto God"* (Philippians 4:6).

You must not be afraid of asking God for anything He has promised you in His words. The grace of God is sufficient to help you get every good thing no matter the economic situation of the world or the failures of the men of science. If the word of God promised you healing, deliverance and prosperity, believe it.

> "[7]*And the LORD appeared unto Abram, and said, Unto thy seed will I give this land: and there builded he an altar unto the LORD, who appeared unto him"* (Genesis 12:7).

> "[15]*For all the land which thou seest, to thee will I give it, and to thy seed forever"* (Genesis 13:15).

> "[7]*And I will establish my covenant between me and thee and thy seed after thee in their generations for an everlasting covenant, to be a God unto thee, and to thy seed after thee.* [8]*And I will give unto thee, and to thy seed after thee, the land wherein thou art a stranger, all the land of Canaan, for an everlasting possession; and I will be their God"* (Genesis 17:7-8).

Abraham and his seeds were outside the land of Canaan when God promised to give them the land as an inheritance. He saw the land and God promised to give them the land forever. At the age of ninety-nine years, God re-emphasized

His promise to Abraham and promised to fulfill it. That's why you should trust God when He has promised you healing, deliverance, prosperity and child bearing, no matter how old you are or how long it takes. As long as you believe God, no matter the circumstance, you will receive an answer. The land promised to Abraham, and his seed was in the hands of Israel's worst enemies at the time Israel left Egypt.

> "[16]*And it came to pass, as we went to prayer, a certain damsel possessed with a spirit of divination met us, which brought her masters much gain by soothsaying:* [17]*The same followed Paul and us, and cried, saying, These men are the servants of the most high God, which shew unto us the way of salvation.* [18]*And this did she many days. But Paul, being grieved, turned and said to the spirit, I command thee in the name of Jesus Christ to come out of her. And he came out the same hour.* [19]*And when her masters saw that the hope of their gains was gone, they caught Paul and Silas, and drew them into the marketplace unto the rulers*" (Acts 16:16-19).

The witches and wizards, occult grand masters may have swallowed your destiny. They may be making gains through your brain, womb or any part of your organs in their covens and altars. Hannah was once a barren woman. Her womb was shut up and her adversary provoked her, insulted her. The womb of everything you do on earth may be shut up. She wept day and night, year after year until she found God's promise.

Have you been surrounded by witches and wizards? I want to remind you that the same thing happened to Elijah until he went into prayers. Allies of power enemies once surrounded Jehoshaphat and he went to God. Daniel's colleagues hated him with great passion and set him up to be eaten by hungry lions. Peter was once locked up in prison. So, no matter what you are going through, great people of God have suffered worst things. The good news is that there is a promise for your deliverance. God has made provision for your complete freedom through His Word.

"[32]And ye shall know the truth, and the truth shall make you free. [33]They answered him, We be Abraham's seed, and were never in bondage to any man: how sayest thou, Ye shall be made free? [34]Jesus answered them, Verily, verily, I say unto you, Whosoever committeth sin is the servant of sin. [35]And the servant abideth not in the house forever: but the Son abideth ever. [36]If the Son therefore shall make you free, ye shall be free indeed"(John 8:32-36).

They answered him, *"We be Abraham's seed, and were never in bondage to any man: how sayest thou, ye shall be made free? Jesus answered them, verily, verily, I say unto you, whosoever, committed sin is the servant of sin. And the servant abideth not in the house forever but the son abideth ever. If the son shall therefore make you free, ye shall be free indeed."*

Goliath was determined to finish the children of Israel. You may have a Goliath in your place of work, family, your body as sickness, God has promised to deliver you. Pharaoh vowed to keep the children of Israel in bondage for life but they have a promise covering their deliverance from every enemy. No enemy has the right to keep you too long if you are born again. The red sea was determined not to give way to the children of Israel. They were cut off from God's promises, provisions and inheritance. God delivered them from Egypt, divided their Red sea because of his promise. The entire first born of Egypt died at mid night for their sake. No problem or power can keep you under bondage forever. If only you can pray, your enemies will bow in this program. You will experience a Passover and a move to another level of life.

"[6]The LORD our God spake unto us in Horeb, saying, Ye have dwelt long enough in this mount: [7]Turn you, and take your journey, and go to the mount of the Amorites, and unto all the places nigh thereunto, in the plain, in the hills, and in the vale, and in the south, and by the sea side, to the land of the Canaanites, and unto Lebanon, unto the great river, the river Euphrates. [8]Behold, I have set the land before you: go in and possess the land which the LORD sware unto

your fathers, Abraham, Isaac, and Jacob, to give unto them and to their seed after them" (Deuteronomy 1:6-8).

"[35]And the same day, when the even was come, he saith unto them, Let us pass over unto the other side" (Mark 4:35).

It is not God's will for you to remain in bondage, problem or one level of life too long. This prayer program will take you into a journey of freedom. You need to re-possess your health, wealth, etc. You may have been suffering in the wilderness with all manner of lack, poverty and death of all kind. God can provide in the desert and renew a life that is about to give up the ghost.

"[17]And God heard the voice of the lad; and the angel of God called to Hagar out of heaven, and said unto her, What aileth thee, Hagar? fear not; for God hath heard the voice of the lad where he is. [18]Arise, lift up the lad, and hold him in thine hand; for I will make him a great nation. [19]And God opened her eyes, and she saw a well of water; and she went, and filled the bottle with water, and gave the lad drink" (Genesis 21:17-19).

You may be abandoned; deceived by loved ones to die but if you can pray in this program, God will deliver you. You may be spiritually blind; God will open your eye to see abundant prosperity. You will be linked up to divine wealth. But you need to believe in God's promises and provisions. In the wilderness, the children of Israel met bitter water but when they cried unto God their waters was made sweet.

"[23]And when they came to Marah, they could not drink of the waters of Marah, for they were bitter: therefore the name of it was called Marah. [24]And the people murmured against Moses, saying, What shall we drink? [25]And he cried unto the LORD; and the LORD shewed him a tree, which when he had cast into the waters, the waters were made sweet: there he made for them a statute and an ordinance, and there he proved them" (Exodus 15:23-25).

Your life may not be better now but God will turn your water into sweet honey.

DIVINE PROVISION

If you need deliverance, God will provide for you. If you need healing, your healing will come. The wall of Jericho may be standing before you. All your enemies may have vowed never to let you go. Your life may be full of sorrow, bitterness, confusion, lack, sickness and diseases, if you believe God's provision, all your enemies must bow. The Amorites believed that the land of Canaan was their ancestral home. They vowed never to vacate the land of promise. They were determined to resist any attempt by Israel to enter their promised land. The children of Israel based their claim on God's promises and provision. They were determined to possess the land despite all oppositions on their way. In the face of all oppositions, God reassured the children of Israel and stated again his covenant promise and provision of the land. (*See* Deuteronomy 30:1-10)

If God promised you anything, believe him because He is faithful to fulfill all his promises.

> *"And the LORD gave unto Israel all the land which he sware to give unto their fathers; and they possessed it, and dwelt therein. And the LORD gave them rest round about, according to all that he sware unto their fathers: and there stood not a man of all their enemies before them; the LORD delivered all their enemies into their hand. There failed not ought of any good thing which the LORD had spoken unto the house of Israel; all came to pass"* (Joshua 21:43-45).

Not even death, the devil can stand against God's word. His promises are yea and Amen. If you will remain faithful to his promises, he will provide for you and deliver you until your life will be freed from all enemies.

God is faithful to fulfill all his promises.

> *"Then the children of Judah came unto Joshua in Gilgal: and Caleb the son of Jephunneh the Kenezite said unto him, Thou knowest the thing that the LORD said unto Moses the man of God concerning me and*

thee in Kadeshbarnea. Forty years old was I when Moses the servant of the LORD sent me from Kadeshbarnea to espy out the land; and I brought him word again as it was in mine heart. Nevertheless my brethren that went up with me made the heart of the people melt: but I wholly followed the LORD my God. And Moses sware on that day, saying, Surely the land whereon thy feet have trodden shall be thine inheritance, and thy children's for ever, because thou hast wholly followed the LORD my God. And now, behold, the LORD hath kept me alive, as he said, these forty and five years, even since the LORD spake this word unto Moses, while the children of Israel wandered in the wilderness: and now, lo, I am this day fourscore and five years old. As yet I am as strong this day as I was in the day that Moses sent me: as my strength was then, even so is my strength now, for war, both to go out, and to come in. Now therefore give me this mountain, whereof the LORD spake in that day; for thou heardest in that day how the Anakims were there, and that the cities were great and fenced: if so be the LORD will be with me, then I shall be able to drive them out, as the LORD said. And Joshua blessed him, and gave unto Caleb the son of Jephunneh Hebron for an inheritance" (Joshua 14:6-13).

God made promise to Caleb and after forty years, he was kept alive to receive the fulfillments. He came to the land that God promised to give him. He did not inherit or possessed his possession until he asked. If you don't asked, you will not receive what God has provided for you. God anointed David but Saul refused to allow him rule. God promised to save him from all his enemies but he has to pray in times of danger. His enemies fought him daily, oppressed him frequently, trying to swallow him up. They twisted his word conspired against him but he put his confidence in God.

"What time I am afraid, I will trust in thee. In God I will praise his word, in God I have put my trust; I will not fear what flesh can do unto me... Thou tellest my

wanderings: put thou my tears into thy bottle: are they not in thy book?" (Psalms 56:3-4, 8).

"In God will I praise His Word: in the LORD will I praise his Word. In God have I put my trust: I will not be afraid what man can do unto me" (Psalms 56:10-11).

When there is a promise, wise people pray but the unwise postpone their prayer till the master of the house has risen up and shut the door before they start knocking.

"Strive to enter in at the strait gate: for many, I say unto you, will seek to enter in, and shall not be able. When once the master of the house is risen up, and hath shut to the door, and ye begin to stand without, and to knock at the door, saying, Lord, Lord, open unto us; and he shall answer and say unto you, I know you not whence ye are: Then shall ye begin to say, We have eaten and drunk in thy presence, and thou hast taught in our streets. But he shall say, I tell you, I know you not whence ye are; depart from me, all ye workers of iniquity. There shall be weeping and gnashing of teeth, when ye shall see Abraham, and Isaac, and Jacob, and all the prophets, in the kingdom of God, and you yourselves thrust out" (Luke 13:24-28).

We are all in battle and our triumph or defeat is dependent in our attitude at the hour of battle. Believers are to seek for God's mercy in times of trials (Psalms 136:1-26). After our salvation, we must give prayers first place early every morning and at all times until the enemies bows. Your prayers must be in faith believing God for impossibilities. Believers should trust God and believe God because their tears are preserved in God's bottles. Our cries to God cannot be in vain.

"And he said unto Jesus, Lord, remember me when thou comest into thy kingdom" (Luke 23:42).

"And he said, let me go, for the day breaketh. And he said, I will not let thee go, except thou bless me" (Genesis 32:26).

You must cry for salvation, for help, deliverance and change. David faced great problems but the promise of God kept him until he fulfilled his destiny.

"For David, after he had served his own generation by the will of God, fell on sleep, and was laid unto his fathers, and saw corruption" (Acts 13:36).

You must not accept defeat, any problem until you fulfill your destiny and make it to heaven.

GOD PROMISE, POWER AND VICTORY

Paul described our problems on earth as light afflictions, which cannot and supposed not to destroy a true child of God.

> *"Again, think ye that we excuse ourselves unto you? we speak before God in Christ: but we do all things, dearly beloved, for your edifying"* (2 Corinthians 12:19).

> *"For, behold, the Lord, the LORD of hosts, doth take away from Jerusalem and from Judah the stay and the staff, the whole stay of bread, and the whole stay of water, The mighty man, and the man of war, the judge, and the prophet, and the prudent, and the ancient"* (Isaiah 3:1-2).

As long as you are here on earth trying to do the right thing, the witches and wizards who believe that the earth is their territory will be energized by the spirit of the age to fire strange arrows into your life. They may attack you with the fires of sickness, poverty, deception, slander, conspiracy, division, contention, strife, criticism and betrayer. It may be a fire of persecution, affliction, oppression, slavery, tribulations, trail, injustice and denial of fundamental human rights, whatever you are going through now; there is a promise of a higher power to stop it. If your problem is coming from the powers in the waters, God promised to be with you, it will not overflow you. If it is from the fire, the promise say, it will not burn you (*See* Daniel 3:19-30).

Not even satanic flames shall be allowed to destroy you in vain. Though affliction may come from all sides, but God's promise will continue to stand greater than any affliction. The Lord will deliver you from them all. A day is coming, during or after this program when you will look for your problems and will not see any trace of them.

God's promises and His power of deliverance are the inheritance of all believers.

"And the Lord shall deliver me from every evil work, and will preserve me unto his heavenly kingdom: to whom be glory for ever and ever. Amen" (2 Timothy 4:18).

"There hath no temptation taken you but such as is common to man: but God is faithful, who will not suffer you to be tempted above that ye are able; but will with the temptation also make a way to escape, that ye may be able to bear it" (1 Corinthians 10:13).

God never leaves us alone to fight against the tempter and his temptations in our natural strength. He promised to help us and deliver us from every evil works, to preserve us unto his heavenly kingdom. He promised not to allow us to suffer from any temptation that is above us. Whatever you are going through now is under God's power. There is a promise of victory attached to every problem in the life of a believer. What you need to do is to be a believer before you start praying. As you resist the devil, your problems in this program, the sustaining grace of God will appear for your deliverance.

"For in that he himself hath suffered being tempted, he is able to succour them that are tempted" (Hebrews 2:18).

"Neither is there any creature that is not manifest in his sight: but all things are naked and opened unto the eyes of him with whom we have to do. Seeing then that we have a great high priest that is passed into the heavens, Jesus the Son of God, let us hold fast our profession. For we have not an high priest which cannot be touched with the feeling of our infirmities; but was in all points tempted like as we are, yet without sin. Let us therefore come boldly unto the throne of grace, that we may obtain mercy, and find grace to help in time of need" (Hebrews 4:13-16).

Jesus has passed through every trials and he is able to deliver anyone in trouble from whatsoever trouble. Once you start praying as you repent, confess and forsake your sins, your enemies will be disgraced. Prayers of believers bring Jesus into the battlefield of our life. Without His presence, we cannot walk at liberty without being harmed, defeated by the wicked spirit and evil people on earth. When the enemy touches us, Jesus is touched, when there is storm we need to awake Christ through prayers.

> *"Finally, brethren, whatsoever things are true, whatsoever things are honest, whatsoever things are just, whatsoever things are pure, whatsoever things are lovely, whatsoever things are of good report; if there be any virtue, and if there be any praise, think on these things"* (Philippians 4:8).

To attract deliverance into your life now, seek for truth, honest life, live just, pure with love. Do things that will bring good report and praise to the name of God. Resist the devils temptations, separate from tempters and temptresses, close every evil channel through which the temptation is coming and pray for God's keeping power and sustaining grace. Your victory is sure as you obey God's word and pray the prayer in this book.

GENERAL PRAYERS

You can pray these general prayers as many times as possible. These prayer points focus on expanding your blessings; attracting new blessings and purging your problems. I believe that as you pray, your prayers will give birth to new things, open your heavens and attract divine unmerited favor until all your enemy bows.

> *"And I will stretch out my hand, and smite Egypt with all my wonders which I will do in the midst thereof: and after that he will let you go"* (Exodus 3:20).

> *"Not because I desire a gift: but I desire fruit that may abound to your account. But I have all, and abound: I am full, having received of Epaphroditus the things which were sent from you, an odor of a sweet smell, a sacrifice acceptable, well pleasing to God. But my God shall supply all your need according to his riches in glory by Christ Jesus"* (Philippians 4:17-19).

> *"For the LORD God is a sun and shield: the LORD will give grace and glory: no good thing will he withhold from them that walk uprightly"* (Psalms 84:11).

In few hours from now, as you pray the prayers below, your level will change and you can never remain the same.

PRAYER POINTS

1. Owners of evil loads in my life, appear, carry your loads, in the name of Jesus.

2. Blood of Jesus, flow into my life and deliver me from every evil load, in the name of Jesus.

3. I command every evil load in my life to drop by force, in the name of Jesus.

4. Fire of God, burn to ashes every evil load in my life, in the name of Jesus.

5. Any invisible hand stealing from my life, I cut you off by force, in the name of Jesus.

6. Every enemy of my deliverance, be exposed and be disgraced, in the name of Jesus.

7. Blood of Jesus, speak me out of every trouble, in the name of Jesus.

8. Any evil personality attacking my life in my dreams, be disgraced forever, in the name of Jesus.

9. Any evil thing that has married me, you are wicked, die, in the name of Jesus.

10. Any evil personality controlling my life, I cut off your existence, in the name of Jesus.

11. Every problem in my life, gather yourself together and die, in the name of Jesus.

12. Every hidden enemy of my life, be exposed and be disgraced, in the name of Jesus.

13. Any mountain of problem standing between my greatness and I, disappear forever, in the name of Jesus.

14. Any power postponing my deliverance, wherever you are, die, in the name of Jesus.

15. Every problem that has woken up with me this morning, you will not go to bed with me, die now, in the name of Jesus.

16. I command every organ of my body to receive full deliverance, in the name of Jesus.

17. Any evil eye monitoring my destiny, be blinded, in the name of Jesus.

18. Blood of Jesus, quench every strange fire burning in my life, in the name of Jesus.

19. Any evil movement all over the world against my life, be demobilized, in the name of Jesus.

20. Every book, satanic files, against my life, catch fire, burn to ashes, in the name of Jesus.

21. I recover double every good thing I had ever lost in life, in the name of Jesus.

22. Every stubborn enemy in the battlefield of my life, what are you still doing, die, in the name of Jesus.

23. Every evil support against my life, be withdrawn by force, in the name of Jesus.

24. Blood of Jesus, flow into my life and destroy my captivity, in the name of Jesus.

25. Every yoke of bondage in my life, break to pieces, in the name of Jesus.

26. Let the backbone of my enemy begin to break by force, in the name of Jesus.

27. O Lord, arise and take me away from devils camp, in the name of Jesus.

28. Every dream of defeats in my life, be converted to victory, in the name of Jesus.

29. I lift every satanic embargo placed against my life, in the name of Jesus.

30. Any evil leg that has ever walked into my life, walk out, in the name of Jesus.

31. Any power that is reviving my problems, be disgraced unto death, in the name of Jesus.

32. Every arrow of shame, disgrace and reproach in my life, backfire, in the name of Jesus.

33. Fire of God, burn to ashes every disease germ in my life, in the name of Jesus.

34. Every enemy of my deliverance, you are finished, die by fire, in the name of Jesus.

35. Any battle going on against my life, end to my favor, in the name of Jesus.

36. Let every dark thing in my life disappear by force, in the name of Jesus.

37. Any witchcraft animal living inside me, die, in the name of Jesus.

38. Any evil program going on against my life, be terminated, in the name of Jesus.

39. Every weakness in my life, be converted to strength, in the name of Jesus.

40. I walk out from the camp of the defeated ones, in the name of Jesus.

41. Any evil king or queen sitting upon my inheritance, be unseated by death, in the name of Jesus.

42. Any evil personality living inside me, come out and die, in the name of Jesus.

43. Any demon on suicide mission against my life, come out, die alone, in the name of Jesus.

44. I command the earth to open and swallow my problems, in the name of Jesus.

45. Any serpent in the garden of my life, come out and die, in the name of Jesus.

46. Every enemy of my peace, victory on earth, receive destructions, in the name of Jesus.

47. I terminate the life of my problems, in the name of Jesus.

48. Every weapon of the enemy against my life, be destroyed, in the name of Jesus.

49. I command my enemies to make mistakes that will favor me, in the name of Jesus.

50. Every enemy of my promotion and deliverance, be disgraced, in the name of Jesus.

51. Any witch or wizard that has vowed to waste my life, be wasted, in the name of Jesus.

52. Let the earthquake and let my deliverance appear by force, in the name of Jesus.

53. Let darkness in any area of my life disappear, in the name of Jesus.

54. Any power contending with my joy and peace, die, in the name of Jesus.

55. O Lord, arise and re-organize my life to your glory, in the name of Jesus.

56. Any power attacking my handwork, receive double destruction, in the name of Jesus.

57. Let every damage my life has ever suffered receive divine repair, in the name of Jesus.

58. I recover double every opportunity I have ever lost, in the name of Jesus.

59. I command all the supporters of my problems to withdraw by force, in the name of Jesus.

60. Any power expanding my problems, die without delay, in the name of Jesus.

61. Any power that has arrested my progress, release it now, in the name of Jesus.

62. Every work of the devil in my life, be terminated, in the name of Jesus.

63. O Lord, arise and deliver my hijacked destiny, in the name of Jesus.

64. Let the powers that activate evil work fail in my life, in the name of Jesus.

65. I command my diverted progress to come back by force, in the name of Jesus.

66. Let all satanic angels contending with my destiny be disgraced, in the name of Jesus.

67. I break and loose myself from every satanic curse and covenants, in the name of Jesus.

68. Any witchcraft property in my life, catch fire, burn to ashes, in the name of Jesus.

69. I command every promise of God to manifest in my life, in the name of Jesus.

70. I reject every evil prophecy and visions in my life, in the name of Jesus.

71. I command my life to move forward by fire, in the name of Jesus.

72. Any satanic traffic warder standing against me, die, in the name of Jesus.

73. Every unprofitable load in my life, drop by force, in the name of Jesus.

74. You my personal stronghold, collapse by thunder in the name of Jesus.

75. Any shame distributor assigned against my life, die with your shame, in the name of Jesus.

76. Blood of Jesus, speak me out of every trouble, in the name of Jesus.

77. Any arrow of infirmity fired into any area of my life, backfire, in the name of Jesus.

78. Every demon of late progress in my life, I cast you out, in the name of Jesus.

79. Let every oppressor in my life be oppressed unto death, in the name of Jesus.

80. Any satanic prayer going on against me, back fire, in the name of Jesus.

81. I scatter unto shame every satanic re-enforcement against me, in the name of Jesus.

82. Let the helpers of my enemies be manipulated to my favor, in the name of Jesus.

83. Let the strength of my enemies be broken to pieces, in the name of Jesus.

84. You my problems, receive double destruction, in the name of Jesus.

85. Let the brain of all the powers behind my problem receive confusion forever, in the name of Jesus.

86. O Lord, empower me with explosive breakthroughs, in the name of Jesus.

87. Every seed of sin in my life, die, in the name of Jesus.

88. Blood of Jesus, repurchase me from every disease's captivity, in the name of Jesus.

89. Let the power of God break every spiritual prison and deliver me, in the name of Jesus.

90. Any evil movement in my body, stop and die, in the name of Jesus.

91. Any power postponing my healing and deliverance, die, in the name of Jesus.

92. Any strange fire, traveling in my body, be quenched, in the name of Jesus.

93. Blood of Jesus, speak death unto every infirmity in my body, in the name of Jesus.

94. Every enemy of my healing and deliverance, die, in the name of Jesus.

95. Let the pillar of witchcraft in my life be uprooted, in the name of Jesus.

96. Every satanic embargo placed against my healing, be lifted, in the name of Jesus.

97. Any evil sacrifice offered against my healing; expire, in the name of Jesus.

98. Any power attacking my health in the dream, die, in the name of Jesus.

99. Any evil covenant hindering my healing, break, in the name of Jesus.

100. I break and loose myself from every curse against my destiny, in the name of Jesus.

101. Holy Ghost fire, burn to ashes every disease germ in my body, in the name of Jesus.

102. Any organ of my life, captured by sickness and disease, be released, in the name of Jesus.

103. Any power defiling my beauty, die by force, in the name of Jesus.

104. I command all the powers behind my suffering to die, in the name of Jesus.

105. Every messenger of pains in my body, carry your message, in the name of Jesus.

106. I break the backbone of every problem in my life, in the name of Jesus.

107. Every demonic wound in any area of my life, receive healing, in the name of Jesus.

108. I shake off every sickness in my body, in the name of Jesus.

You my head, body, soul and spirit, discharge every problem in you, in the name of Jesus.

WARFARE PRAYERS SECTION

CHAPTER OVERVIEW

Prayers in this section include prayers to preserve your job and destiny, footballers, busy people, great changes, immediate change, divine guidance, change of job, prevail in job seeking, to be successful in your job, for sportsmen and women, top employment, wisdom to become self-employed, to be gainfully employed, get a better job, move into a new place, excel above your masters, excel in job interview, force your enemies out of your life, to force your enemies to bow, move god into action open closed doors, release your burdens and prayers to win in competitions.

PRAYER TOPICS ON THIS SECTION

PRAYER TO PRESERVE YOUR JOB AND DESTINY

It is rather unfortunate that most people do not strive to preserve their jobs or destiny through prayers. They forget that Satan's job is to keep people out of job, frustrate destinies and push people out of God's plan and purposes. Satan and his demons are very wicked. But by the power in the blood of Jesus, you are triumphant already. And no weapon formed against you shall prosper, in the name of Jesus.

> "[18]*The Spirit of the Lord is upon me, because he hath anointed me to preach the gospel to the poor; he hath sent me to heal the brokenhearted, to preach deliverance to the captives, and recovering of sight to the blind, to set at liberty them that are bruised"* (Luke 4:18).

> "[8]*But if any provide not for his own, and especially for those of his own house, he hath denied the faith, and is worse than an infidel"* (1 Timothy 5:8).

God's power has anointing that breaks satanic bondages, sets captives free and cast out demons. Many people today are poor because they have not believed the gospel that can set them free. Whenever a sick, poor and broken-hearted person hears the gospel, it delivers and repositions that same person to work and earn a living to fulfill his or her destiny.

> "[36]*For David, after he had served his own generation by the will of God, fell on sleep, and was laid unto his fathers, and saw corruption"* (Acts 13:36).

Everyone on earth has a job to do and a destiny to fulfill. Therefore, let no one lead you astray through unbelief.

PRAYER POINTS

1. Father Lord, thank You for my job, in the name of Jesus.

2. Any power that has vowed to take away my job, die, in the name of Jesus.

3. Let the power of God to keep my job fall upon me, in the name of Jesus.

4. Blood of Jesus, speak peace into my job, in the name of Jesus.

5. Any evil personality that has been assigned to take away my job, be frustrated, in the name of Jesus.

6. Let the grace of God to keep my job manifest in my life, in the name of Jesus.

7. Every evil gang-up to remove me from my office, scatter in shame, in the name of Jesus.

8. O Lord, arise and help me to perform my duties well, in the name of Jesus.

9. Any evil report written against me, be converted to my favor, in the name of Jesus.

10. Blessed Holy Ghost, fight for me in my office, in the name of Jesus.

11. Any man, woman or power that is sitting upon my promotion, be unseated, in the name of Jesus.

12. Lord Jesus, destroy every weakness in my life at place of work, in the name of Jesus.

13. I command every evil program in my life to depart, in the name of Jesus.

14. O Lord, help me to do my work with ease, in the name of Jesus.

15. Let angels of the living God move me to where enemies cannot see my job, in the name of Jesus.

16. O Lord, do not allow anybody to replace me yet, in the name of Jesus.

17. Holy Ghost fire, burn every evil document written against me, in the name of Jesus.

18. I disallow any case that will surface to cost me my job, in the name of Jesus.

19. Let any sack, evil transfer or suspension letters written for my sake be withdrawn, in the name of Jesus.

20. I withdraw my name from any evil in this organization, in the name of Jesus.

21. Let my enemies make double mistakes that will promote me, in the name of Jesus.

22. Any evil action taken against me in my place of work, be revoked, in the name of Jesus.

23. Any evil decree that is made against my job, be reversed, in the name of Jesus.

24. Any evil mouth speaking against my job, be closed forever, in the name of Jesus.

25. Any evil meeting summoned for my sake, end to my favor, in the name of Jesus.

26. O Lord, use every enemy of my job to promote me, in the name of Jesus.

27. Any evil personality that has vowed to sack me, be dismissed, in the name of Jesus.

28. Let my enemies in the office begin to make mistakes that will promote me, in the name of Jesus.

29. Any evil conversation against my destiny, be reversed to my favor, in the name of Jesus.

30. O Lord, arise and frustrate my challenges in this office, in the name of Jesus.

31. Father Lord, place people that will save my job among the decision makers, in the name of Jesus.

32. Let me find favor before people, who will finally decide my case, in the name of Jesus.

33. Any evil personality prepared to take my job, loose your own job, in the name of Jesus.

34. Blood of Jesus, empower me to stand for truth always, in the name of Jesus.

35. Every enemy of truth in this office, be disgraced, in the name of Jesus.

36. Fire of God, make life uncomfortable for those who are against my job, in the name of Jesus.

37. Any man, woman or power that has vowed to frustrate me in this work, be frustrated, in the name of Jesus.

38. Any evil yoke placed upon me in this office, break to pieces, in the name of Jesus.

39. O Lord, arise and help me to keep my job, in the name of Jesus.

40. Any power that wants me to overstay in this office without promotion, die, in the name of Jesus.

41. O Lord, feed me with the food of champions in my office, in the name of Jesus.

42. Power to retain my job until the end, what are you waiting for? Possess me, in the name of Jesus.

43. Every satanic embargo placed upon my job, be lifted by force, in the name of Jesus.

44. Every evil cry against my job, be silenced, in the name of Jesus.

45. Any witchcraft animal sent to swallow my job, die, in the name of Jesus.

46. Any evil wind blowing against my job, be diverted by force, in the name of Jesus.

47. Any satanic padlock that has been used to lock me out of job, break, in the name of Jesus.

48. Any evil pronouncement against my job, be reversed, in the name of Jesus.

49. Lord Jesus, arise and preserve my job by Your power, in the name of Jesus.

50. Any petition writer that has been assigned to write against me, write to my favor, in the name of Jesus.

51. Let the grace to keep my job locate me, in the name of Jesus.

52. Let the air move to fight for my job's security, in the name of Jesus.

53. Any grand demon that is assigned to work against my job, I cut you off, in the name of Jesus.

54. I fire back every evil arrow fired at my life, in the name of Jesus.

55. Father Lord, use this job to advertise me locally and internationally, in the name of Jesus.

56. Let my job take off from ground level to topmost level, in the name of Jesus.

57. O Lord, command my eagles to fly so high, in the name of Jesus.

58. Let an opportunity that will make me greater than my bosses manifest in my office, in the name of Jesus.

59. Let my life take off from ground heights to greater heights, in the name of Jesus.

60. Any evil bird that is flying against my life, die, in the name of Jesus.

61. I rise above my equals, masters and leaders by force, in the name of Jesus.

62. Any evil personality ruling over my life, be demoted, in the name of Jesus.

63. Let the hand of God move me from where I am now to where I am supposed to be, in the name of Jesus.

64. Any evil eyes monitoring my job, be blinded, in the name of Jesus.

65. Any evil sacrifice that was offered against my life, expire, in the name of Jesus.

66. Blood of Jesus, flow into my job and protect it, in the name of Jesus.

67. Any evil serpent flying against my destiny, die, in the name of Jesus.

68. I bring down evil powers that have risen up against my life, in the name of Jesus.

69. Any household enemy working against my destiny, be disgraced, in the name of Jesus.

70. Any power bringing me down, die, in the name of Jesus.

71. O Lord, give me divine wings to fly high, in the name of Jesus.

72. Power to stop devil and his works, possess me, in the name of Jesus.

73. I receive the anointing to go wherever my job takes me, in the name of Jesus.

74. I receive the power to do all kinds of jobs perfectly to God's glory, in the name of Jesus.

75. Any power attacking my handiwork from the waters and air, die, in the name of Jesus.

76. No power can restrain me to local level only, in the name of Jesus.

77. Let the anointing for international meetings and appointments possess me now, in the name of Jesus.

78. O Lord, empower me to accomplish difficult jobs to Your own glory, in the name of Jesus.

79. I am empowered to rise above all my rivalries, in the name of Jesus.

80. Blood of Jesus, flow from above to the waters, seas and land for my sake, in the name of Jesus.

81. Let grand demons bow to my commands, in the name of Jesus.

82. I will not stand below my divine level, in the name of Jesus.

83. Fire of God from above, possess me, in the name of Jesus.

84. I receive heavenly anointing to succeed by force, in the name of Jesus.

85. O Lord, bless me in all areas of life, in the name of Jesus.

86. Lord Jesus, empower me to receive the nine gifts of the Holy Ghost, in the name of Jesus.

87. I command the whole creature to bow and serve me forever, in the name of Jesus.

88. O Lord, control all my movements, in the name of Jesus.

89. Any evil force in-charge of the air, you must respect my interests, in the name of Jesus.

90. Every evil in the air, I command you to release all my blessings, in the name of Jesus.

91. Let the atmosphere gather my blessings and hand them to me, in the name of Jesus.

92. I reverse every evil pronouncement made against me, in the name of Jesus.

93. Any witch or wizard that is using the heavenlies against me, make mistakes to my favor, in the name of Jesus.

94. O Lord, arise and help me to make good achievements, in the name of Jesus.

95. Let the sun, moon and the stars refuse to respond to my enemies, in the name of Jesus.

96. I command the elements and their powers to favor me forever, in the name of Jesus.

97. Any occult personality using the heavens against me, fail for my sake, in the name of Jesus.

98. I command principalities and all satanic hosts to bow before me, in the name of Jesus.

99. I speak death to my problems from the third heaven, in the name of Jesus.

100. Every problem in my life, what are you waiting for? Die, in the name of Jesus.

101. I receive power to prosper above all human imaginations, in the name of Jesus.

102. I command my prosperity to locate me now, in the name of Jesus.

103. Any evil personality that wants me to die, be disgraced, in the name of Jesus.

104. Any evil plan against me, be exposed, in the name of Jesus.

105. O Lord, empower me to escape from troubles, in the name of Jesus.

106. Any spirit of failure assigned to my life, be frustrated, in the name of Jesus.

107. Any arrow of poverty and debt in my life, come out now and go back to your sender, in the name of Jesus.

108. Any property of witchcraft in my life, catch fire and expire, in the name of Jesus.

109. Any evil seed planted for my sake, die, in the name of Jesus.

110. O Lord, give me a position on earth that will glorify You, in the name of Jesus.

111. Father Lord, develop my brain to the highest capacity, in the name of Jesus.

112. Let my mental storehouse think out something that will help my generation, in the name of Jesus.

113. I command my destiny to escape from limitations and bondage, in the name of Jesus.

114. Let my past evil records disappear forever, in the name of Jesus.

115. I command my past problems to die forever, in the name of Jesus.

116. Any evil past cannot stop my present and future advancements, in the name of Jesus.

117. Heavenly Father, heal me and keep me healthy by the stripes of Jesus, in the name of Jesus.

118. Any power or creature assigned to force me out of this earth before my time, die, in the name of Jesus.

119. Let the angels of God be my security forever, in the name of Jesus.

120. Any power that refuses to allow me to fulfill my destiny shall die, in the name of Jesus.

201. Blood of Jesus, speak me into the people that matters in this world, in the name of Jesus.

202. Let the leaders of the world, both now and in the future, favor me, in the name of Jesus.

203. I command every door locked against me to open at my command, in the name of Jesus.

204. O Lord, bless me with silver and gold, in the name of Jesus.

205. I release my children and offspring from every kind of bondage, in the name of Jesus.

206. Any yoke of sin in my life, break, in the name of Jesus.

207. Father Lord, connect me with good people on earth, in the name of Jesus.

208. I receive the power of God to make heaven at last, in the name of Jesus.

209. Any evil plan to overthrow my faith in Christ, be aborted, in the name of Jesus.

210. I fire back every arrow of sickness and disease in my life, in the name of Jesus.

211. Anointing to carry people along in anything I do, possess me, in the name of Jesus.

212. I walk out from institutional captivity, even from the Garden of Eden, in the name of Jesus.

213. Lord Jesus, walk me back to my paradise that is free of serpents, in the name of Jesus.

214. Let my life be too hot for Satan and his entire agents now and forever, in the name of Jesus.

215. Let my life be a blessing to all and not a curse, in the name of Jesus.

216. O Lord, use me to stop Satan like Phillip did in Samaria, in the name of Jesus.

217. Wherever my handiwork will be seen, it shall work more than my presence, in the name of Jesus.

218. Let my work dominate the internet by force, in the name of Jesus.

219. Let the heaven advertise my handiwork by force, in the name of Jesus.

220. Everywhere trouble is raging, O Lord, use me to silence it, in the name of Jesus.

221. I receive power to hear and see, both physical and spiritually, in the name of Jesus.

222. Any begging spirit in me, be limited to begging God alone, in the name of Jesus.

223. O Lord, teach me and empower me to pray rightly, in the name of Jesus.

224. Evil cases against people all over the world, I break you to release your captives, in the name of Jesus.

225. By the anointing that breaks every yoke, I break my yokes, in the name of Jesus.

226. I receive power to break every yoke all over the world, in the name of Jesus.

227. O Lord, take my handwork to all over the world to bless people, in the name of Jesus.

228. I shall rise and shine above others by the grace of God, in the name of Jesus.

229. Let my angels of blessing bless me on continual basis, in the name of Jesus.

230. As I lay down any time, my enemies must surrender, in the name of Jesus.

231. Holy Ghost fire, burn every demonic water in my life, in the name of Jesus.

232. Let all the creatures surrender to my God whether they like it or not, in the name of Jesus.

233. I refuse to find fault with God and His Word, in the name of Jesus.

234. O God, use me as You have never before, in the name of Jesus.

235. Lord Jesus, impart in me Your nature fully and double it, in the name of Jesus.

236. I command all idols of devil in my life to burn to ashes, in the name of Jesus.

237. Let the work of flesh and devil's character have no place in my life, in the name of Jesus.

238. O Lord, bless my family and help them to stand with You until the end, in the name of Jesus.

239. Let the voice of God advertise all that I do on earth, in the name of Jesus.

240. I overcome every Delilah, Jezebel and their likes all over the world, in the name of Jesus.

241. As I walk, I shall not fall or stumble, in the name of Jesus.

242. Let God reign and rule over my life forever, in the name of Jesus.

243. My departure out of this world shall be glorious, in the name of Jesus.

244. O Lord, overthrow every evil government on earth and replace them with good ones, in the name of Jesus.

245. Let my master Jesus reign over the earth physically through His appointed saints, in the name of Jesus.

246. I receive God's mandate to make the world a better place, in the name of Jesus.

247. Let God arise and let His enemies scatter, in the name of Jesus.

248. Blood of Jesus, flow into the air, sea and lands for my sake, in the name of Jesus.

249. Let my children make it more than I did by fire, in the name of Jesus.

250. I receive every answer to my prayers on earth, in the name of Jesus.

251. Sweet Father, sweet Jesus, sweet Holy Ghost, make my life perfect and sweet on earth, in the name of Jesus.

252. Let my name be filled with noble deeds and divine achievements, in the name of Jesus.

253. I command the whole earth to surrender to my creator forever, in the name of Jesus.

254. Yokes must be broken by force as I minister anywhere I go, in the name of Jesus.

255. Father Lord, thank You for Your answers to my prayers, in the name of Jesus.

256. Satan, get lost and as you go, go with all your loads in my life and on earth, in the name of Jesus.

257. I receive the grace to be among the best brains on earth, in the name of Jesus.

258. Any evil altar on earth against my life, perish with the ones outside the earth for my safe, in the name of Jesus.

259. Blood of Jesus, silence every evil blood crying against me, in the name of Jesus.

260. I walk into divine liberty forever and ever, in the name of Jesus.

PRAYER FOR FOOTBALLERS

Whatever achievements you are able to make today as a footballer are because of God's mercy. The reason you are still playing and being favored as a footballer, is because God has favored you first, not because you are the best. It will be a great mistake to start imagining that you are the best. Many people are more talented out there. But God favored you. So the best thing you can do is to thank God and remain in prayers in order to retain the favor of God over your life and career. It is also wise to give your life to Christ now. Without Him, every achievement would be worthless.

> *"[6]Do ye thus requite the LORD, O foolish people and unwise? Is not he thy father that hath bought thee? hath he not made thee, and established thee?"* (Deuteronomy 32:6).

> *"[6]Jesus saith unto him, I am the way, the truth, and the life: no man cometh unto the Father, but by me"* (John 14:6).

> *"[28]Come unto me, all ye that labor and are heavy laden, and I will give you rest"* (Matthew 11:28).

When you surrender your life to Christ, He makes you His best, promotes your talent and makes you to last longer than other footballers. From today, I prophesy that you will score not only more goal goals, but also the best goals. You will be the most capped player in your club and country. You will be the best among your peers and remain healthy and fit even to your old age in the name of Jesus.

> *"[9]Because thou hast made the LORD, which is my refuge, even the most High, thy habitation; [10]There shall no evil befall thee, neither shall any plague*

come nigh thy dwelling. [11]For he shall give his angels charge over thee, to keep thee in all thy ways. [12]They shall bear thee up in their hands, lest thou dash thy foot against a stone. [13]Thou shalt tread upon the lion and adder: the young lion and the dragon shalt thou trample under feet. [14]Because he hath set his love upon me, therefore will I deliver him: I will set him on high, because he hath known my name. [15]He shall call upon me, and I will answer him: I will be with him in trouble; I will deliver him, and honor him. [16]With long life will I satisfy him, and shew him my salvation" (Psalms 91:9-16).

PRAYER POINTS

1. I command every game to end to my favor and to the glory of God, in the name of Jesus.
2. I will dribble pass all my opponents, in the name of Jesus.
3. I command the legs of my opponents to miss the ball by force, in the name of Jesus.
4. I release ninety minutes perfect defeat to my opponents, in the name of Jesus.
5. Let the angels of God keep balls away from my goal post, in the name of Jesus.
6. I send all attempts on goals from my opponents over the bars, in the name of Jesus.
7. Let the strength of my opponents fail them mysteriously, in the name of Jesus.
8. O Lord, arise and give me an overwhelming victory in this game, in the name of Jesus.
9. I remove the concentration, unity and team spirit of my opponents, in the name of Jesus.
10. O Lord, arise and direct my attempts into my opponent's goal post, in the name of Jesus.
11. I command the opponent's goalkeeper to avoid my strikes like poison, in the name of Jesus.
12. No goalkeeper will catch my shorts at ball, in the name of Jesus.
13. Let my opponents mistakenly pass the ball to me for a score, in the name of Jesus.

14. Anointing to score goals effortlessly without pains and difficulties, possess me now, in the name of Jesus.

15. I kick the ball into the goal area where the goalkeeper's hands can never reach, in the name of Jesus.

16. I must score in any given penalty, in the name of Jesus.

17. Grace of God to score an early and winning goal, possess me, in the name of Jesus.

18. Any enemy that is assigned to stop me in the field, be frustrated, in the name of Jesus.

19. Let the power, talent and spirit of victory of my opponent fail them woefully, in the name of Jesus.

20. Lord Jesus, give me victory that cannot be questioned in this game, in the name of Jesus.

21. I overcome the strength, hope and zeal of my opponent to win, in the name of Jesus.

22. Let the opposing coach make a wrong selection that will favor my team, in the name of Jesus.

PRAYER FOR BUSY PEOPLE

Have you ever noticed that everyone is busy? The question is, what is everyone busy doing? Or who is every busy for? Most busy people are not busy for themselves. That's why they cannot be happy anytime you see them. Majority of the people are busy in suffering while others enjoy the fruits of their labors.

> "[38]*This twenty years have I been with thee; thy ewes and thy she goats have not cast their young, and the rams of thy flock have I not eaten.* [39]*That which was torn of beasts I brought not unto thee; I bare the loss of it; of my hand didst thou require it, whether stolen by day, or stolen by night.* [40]*Thus I was; in the day the drought consumed me, and the frost by night; and my sleep departed from mine eyes.* [41]*Thus have I been twenty years in thy house; I served thee fourteen years for thy two daughters, and six years for thy cattle: and thou hast changed my wages ten times*" (Genesis 31:38-41).

> "[16]*And it came to pass, as we went to prayer, a certain damsel possessed with a spirit of divination met us, which brought her masters much gain by soothsaying:* [17] *The same followed Paul and us, and cried, saying, These men are the servants of the most high God, which shew unto us the way of salvation.* [18]*And this did she many days. But Paul, being grieved, turned and said to the spirit, I command thee in the name of Jesus Christ to come out of her. And he came out the same hour.* [19]*And when her masters saw that the hope of their gains was gone, they caught Paul and Silas, and drew them into the marketplace unto the rulers*" (Acts 16:16-19).

Jacob was busy working for Laban while Laban was on the other end enjoying the fruits of his labors. Many occult grandmasters are spiritually siphoning the labors of their ignorant victims on earth. No one is expected to be idle or lazy. But most importantly, what we must be busy doing at all times is God's will for our lives on earth, in order to fulfill our God's given destiny.

> "[36]*For David, after he had served his own generation by the will of God, fell on sleep, and was laid unto his fathers, and saw corruption*" (Acts 13:36).

> "[22]*And Enoch walked with God after he begat Methuselah three hundred years, and begat sons and daughters:* [23]*And all the days of Enoch were three hundred sixty and five years:* [24]*And Enoch walked with God: and he was not; for God took him*" (Genesis 5:22-24).

Ask God to make you busy for Him and not for self or the devil and his agents. If your job does not give you enough time to commune God, then begin to seek for God's own choice of job for you, where His name alone would be pleased. Our time, money, talent, possession and labor are spent well when they please God at all times and link others to Christ.

PRAYER POINTS

1. O Lord, help me to do all that I am supposed to do for Your will, in the name of Jesus.

2. Any power assigned to keep me busy for nothing, die, in the name of Jesus.

3. I refuse to neglect my personal responsibilities at my busy times, in the name of Jesus.

4. Power to use my busy time to the glory of God, possess me now, in the name of Jesus.

5. I receive anointing not to overlook the things that matter at my busy hours, in the name of Jesus.

6. Blood of Jesus, flow into my foundation and coordinate my life, in the name of Jesus.

7. Let the powers that destroy people at their busy times fail in my case, in the name of Jesus.

8. O Lord, help me to be profitable to Your kingdom at my busy times, in the name of Jesus.

9. Any agent of Satan that has vowed to waste me at my busy times, be wasted, in the name of Jesus.

10. My health will not fail me at my busy times, in the name of Jesus.

11. No part of my life shall be neglected at my busy times, in the name of Jesus.

12. Lord Jesus, help me not to fail or regret my busy times, in the name of Jesus.

13. Father Lord, use me to achieve great things during busy times, in the name of Jesus.

14. Father God, draw me closer to You especially at my busy moments, in the name of Jesus.

15. I receive divine strength to do all that I am expected to do at any given time, in the name of Jesus.

16. I deliver every area of my life from satanic activities, in the name of Jesus.

17. O Lord, help me to fulfill my destiny at any given opportunity, in the name of Jesus.

18. I command frustrations to depart from my life and business, in the name of Jesus.

PRAYER FOR GREAT CHANGES

From the time of birth to the grave is filled with periods of trials, tests and temptations of life. The world is a battlefield. That's why Paul, the Apostle, likened a Christian lifestyle to warfare, battles, fighting and wrestling. Every human is engaged in one battle or another. Unless you begin to resist the devil, you will never experience any good change in your life.

> "[1]*Then was Jesus led up of the Spirit into the wilderness to be tempted of the devil.* [3]*And when the tempter came to him, he said, If thou be the Son of God, command that these stones be made bread* [11]*Then the devil leaveth him, and, behold, angels came and ministered unto him*" (Matthew 4:1, 3, 11).

> "[18]*Wherefore we would have come unto you, even I Paul, once and again; but Satan hindered us*" (1 Thessalonians 2:18).

"[3]*And they said unto him, Thus saith Hezekiah, This day is a day of trouble, and of rebuke, and of blasphemy: for the children are come to the birth, and there is not strength to bring forth*" (Isaiah 37:3).

If you desire great changes to take place in your life, then you must put up great battles against the devil and his agents. There are people on earth, who are making incantations and seeking to destroy people's destiny at all times.

> "[16]*And it came to pass, as we went to prayer, a certain damsel possessed with a spirit of divination met us, which brought her masters much gain by soothsaying…* [19]*And when her masters saw that the*

hope of their gains was gone, they caught Paul and Silas, and drew them into the marketplace unto the rulers" (Acts 16:16).

"[17]I shall see him, but not now: I shall behold him, but not nigh: there shall come a Star out of Jacob, and a Sceptre shall rise out of Israel, and shall smite the corners of Moab, and destroy all the children of Sheth" (Numbers 24:17).

Because of heightened satanic operations, many people's destinies, professions, careers, finances, marriages, etc., have been captured and ruined by devil and his agents.

"[6]And David was greatly distressed; for the people spake of stoning him, because the soul of all the people was grieved, every man for his sons and for his daughters: but David encouraged himself in the LORD his God… [18]And David recovered all that the Amalekites had carried away: and David rescued his two wives. [19]And there was nothing lacking to them, neither small nor great, neither sons nor daughters, neither spoil, nor any thing that they had taken to them: David recovered all. [20]And David took all the flocks and the herds, which they drave before those other cattle, and said, This is David's spoil" (1 Samuel 30:6).

"[1]And afterward Moses and Aaron went in, and told Pharaoh, Thus saith the LORD God of Israel, Let my people go, that they may hold a feast unto me in the wilderness" (Exodus 5:1).

Jabez grew up and discovered that devil had confiscated everything that would make him happy in life, including family wealth. So he started praying for a great change and God heard him and changed his situations. His sorrows became Joy. Jacob also confronted his problems through prayers and God changed his name to Israel.

"[9]And Jabez was more honorable than his brethren: and his mother called his name Jabez, saying,

Because I bare him with sorrow. [10]*And Jabez called on the God of Israel, saying, Oh that thou wouldest bless me indeed, and enlarge my coast, and that thine hand might be with me, and that thou wouldest keep me from evil, that it may not grieve me! And God granted him that which he requested"* (1 Chronicles 4:9-10).

"[24]*And Jacob was left alone; and there wrestled a man with him until the breaking of the day.* [25]*And when he saw that he prevailed not against him, he touched the hollow of his thigh; and the hollow of Jacob's thigh was out of joint, as he wrestled with him.* [26]*And he said, Let me go, for the day breaketh. And he said, I will not let thee go, except thou bless me.* [27]*And he said unto him, What is thy name? And he said, Jacob.* [28]*And he said, Thy name shall be called no more Jacob, but Israel: for as a prince hast thou power with God and with men, and hast prevailed"* (Genesis 32:24-28).

To them that repent and pray for a great change in the name of our Lord Jesus Christ, no difficult condition can remain permanent.

PRAYER POINTS

1. O Lord, empower me to make great changes on earth to Your glory, in the name of Jesus.
2. Every enemy of my greatness on earth, I kill you by force, in the name of Jesus.
3. I receive power to subdue evil kingdoms and glorify God, in the name of Jesus.
4. Every enemy of divine change in my life, be arrested to death, in the name of Jesus.
5. Any satanic blockage against my destiny, be dismantled, in the name of Jesus.
6. O Lord, upgrade my brain and use me to discover hidden things, in the name of Jesus.
7. Let the whole universe be blessed by my discoveries to the glory of God, in the name of Jesus.
8. Father Lord, give me a new breakthrough skill to move the world forward, in the name of Jesus.
9. O Lord, arise and change my situation for the best, in the name of Jesus.
10. Any change in my life that will dethrone the devil, appear, in the name of Jesus.
11. Any evil sacrifice that is offered to stop me from bringing good change on earth, expire, in the name of Jesus.
12. Every enemy of my greatness, be arrested and destroyed, in the name of Jesus.
13. Any strange fire that is burning against my zeal for a great change, be quenched, in the name of Jesus.

14. Let the change that will set captives free begin to come, in the name of Jesus.

15. O Lord, help me to command changes all over the world, in the name of Jesus.

16. Every enemy of divine change in the world, die, in the name of Jesus.

17. Every change that will dethrone devil in the lives of multitudes, appear, in the name of Jesus.

18. Blood of Jesus, use me to bring great changes that will dethrone the devil on earth, in the name of Jesus.

19. Let every manner of godly change begin to take place in my life, in the name of Jesus.

20. Changes that will terminate evil operations, appear by force, in the name of Jesus.

PRAYER FOR AN IMMEDIATE CHANGE

Believers, who have not realized that a Christian life is equated to warfare, fighting and wrestling, settle with anything they see in their lives. They take every evil thing that happens to them as God's will. As a result, devil corrupted all the good plans of God for their lives to suit his own wicked plans for them.

> "[3]*And they said unto him, Thus saith Hezekiah, This day is a day of trouble, and of rebuke, and of blasphemy: for the children are come to the birth, and there is not strength to bring forth*" (Isaiah 37:3).

> "[46]*And they came to Jericho: and as he went out of Jericho with his disciples and a great number of people, blind Bartimæus, the son of Timæus, sat by the highway side begging.* [47]*And when he heard that it was Jesus of Nazareth, he began to cry out, and say, Jesus, thou Son of David, have mercy on me.* [48]*And many charged him that he should hold his peace: but he cried the more a great deal, Thou Son of David, have mercy on me.* [49]*And Jesus stood still, and commanded him to be called. And they call the blind man, saying unto him, Be of good comfort, rise; he calleth thee.* [50]*And he, casting away his garment, rose, and came to Jesus.* [51]*And Jesus answered and said unto him, What wilt thou that I should do unto thee? The blind man said unto him, Lord, that I might receive my sight.* [52]*And Jesus said unto him, Go thy way; thy faith hath made thee whole. And immediately he received his sight, and followed Jesus in the way*" (Mark 10:46-52).

King Hezekiah woke up one day and discovered that God's plan for his life was converted to a day of trouble, rebuke and blasphemy. To some people, they would have accepted the verdict. But Hezekiah rejected it and cried to God for a change. Bartimaeus was under demonic sentence for many years. The devil arrested him, kept him bound as he sat on the highway begging for crumbs for 40 years.

> "[24]*And Jacob was left alone; and there wrestled a man with him until the breaking of the day.* [25]*And when he saw that he prevailed not against him, he touched the hollow of his thigh; and the hollow of Jacob's thigh was out of joint, as he wrestled with him.* [26]*And he said, Let me go, for the day breaketh. And he said, I will not let thee go, except thou bless me.* [27]*And he said unto him, What is thy name? And he said, Jacob.* [28]*And he said, Thy name shall be called no more Jacob, but Israel: for as a prince hast thou power with God and with men, and hast prevailed.* [29]*And Jacob asked him, and said, Tell me, I pray thee, thy name. And he said, Wherefore is it that thou dost ask after my name? And he blessed him there*" (Genesis 32:24-29).

Jacob complained for many years until he decided to pray for a change. Today, many children of God are complaining, without really facing their problems. They forget that they must take their problems to God in prayers so they could receive mercy and deliverance.

> "[21]*So he fled with all that he had; and he rose up, and passed over the river, and set his face toward the mount Gilead...*[36]*And Jacob was wroth, and chode with Laban: and Jacob answered and said to Laban, What is my trespass? What is my sin that thou hast so hotly pursued after me?* [37]*Whereas thou hast searched all my stuff, what hast thou found of all thy household stuff? set it here before my brethren and thy brethren, that they may judge betwixt us both.* [38]*This twenty years have I been with thee; thy ewes and thy she goats have not cast their young, and the rams of thy flock have I not eaten.* [39]*That which was torn of beasts I brought not unto thee; I bare the loss of it; of my hand didst thou require it,*

> *whether stolen by day, or stolen by night.* [40]*Thus I was; in the day the drought consumed me, and the frost by night; and my sleep departed from mine eyes.* [41]*Thus have I been twenty years in thy house; I served thee fourteen years for thy two daughters, and six years for thy cattle: and thou hast changed my wages ten times"* (Genesis 31:21).

When Jacob got tired of remaining at a particular level of life every year, he ran away, separated himself and prayed for a great change. God is calling us to desire for great changes because He wants to take us to greater heights. May you climb to a greater height as you seek God through this prayer program, in the name of Jesus.

> *"And the same day, when the even was come, he saith unto them, Let us pass over to the other side"* (Mark 4:35).

> *"*[6]*The LORD our God spake unto us in Horeb, saying, Ye have dwelt long enough in this mount:* [7]*Turn you, and take your journey, and go to the mount of the Amorites, and unto all the places nigh thereunto, in the plain, in the hills, and in the vale, and in the south, and by the sea side, to the land of the Canaanites, and unto Lebanon, unto the great river, the river Euphrates"* (Deuteronomy 1:6-7).

Until you begin to resist the devil, he will never allow you to go higher. Resist him courageously today, and like the bible said, *"he will flee from you."*

PRAYER POINTS

1. Every evil imagination against my life, be reversed to my favor, in the name of Jesus.
2. Every unprofitable speech going on against my life, be silenced, in the name of Jesus.
3. O Lord, give me a breakthrough that will make me momentously great, in the name of Jesus.
4. I command every Goliath-like enemy in my life to die, in the name of Jesus.
5. Father Lord, arise and take me to the greatest height in life, in the name of Jesus.
6. I convert every reproach and shame in my life to testimonies, in the name of Jesus.
7. I command all my enemies to bow down and begin to serve me, in the name of Jesus.
8. Lord Jesus, bring satanic agents under my foot, in the name of Jesus.
9. Let my promotion rise from the grave and locate me, in the name of Jesus.
10. O Lord, place me in a place where no agents of devil can reach, in the name of Jesus.
11. Let every problem in my life die and die forever, in the name of Jesus.
12. I bring down every evil throne by force, in the name of Jesus.
13. Let my breakthrough supersede every other breakthrough in my generation, in the name of Jesus.

14. I command my blessings to increase on daily basis, in the name of Jesus.
15. Father Lord, increase my finance and material possessions for Your glory, in the name of Jesus.
16. I command activators of evil spells to die forever in my life, in the name of Jesus.
17. Every evil limit that is placed upon my life, disappear, in the name of Jesus.
18. Blood of Jesus, speak my promotion up to the third heaven, in the name of Jesus.
19. Every obstacle that is waiting for me, disappear, in the name of Jesus.
20. Let the change that will occur in my life please God greatly, in the name of Jesus.
21. Every enemy of my change, die forever, in the name of Jesus.

PRAYER FOR DIVINE GUIDANCE

Prayer for guidance is a very important prayer. Choices you make in life can determine your success and greatness or destruction and ruin. They can also determine where you will spend your eternity. When we convince ourselves that we have the capacity to guide ourselves, then ruin and destruction becomes our ultimate end. Anyone, who fails to surrender his life for divine guidance, will definitely end up in sorrow, here on earth and thereafter.

> *"[15]And in those days Peter stood up in the midst of the disciples, and said, (the number of names together were about an hundred and twenty,) [16]Men and brethren, this scripture must needs have been fulfilled, which the Holy Ghost by the mouth of David spake before concerning Judas, which was guide to them that took Jesus. [17]For he was numbered with us, and had obtained part of this ministry. [18]Now this man purchased a field with the reward of iniquity; and falling headlong, he burst asunder in the midst, and all his bowels gushed out. [19]And it was known unto all the dwellers at Jerusalem; insomuch as that field is called in their proper tongue, Aceldama, that is to say, The field of blood. [20]For it is written in the book of Psalms, Let his habitation be desolate, and let no man dwell therein: and his bishoprick let another take"* (Acts 1:15-20).

One of the greatest problems with so many people in this generation is walking by sight and the senses. A carnal and natural mind cannot receive or appreciate any spiritual revelation. It is foolishness to a carnal and covetously blind man. Those, who do not love the truth will be led by strong delusions to believe a lie.

> "[9]*Even him, whose coming is after the working of Satan with all power and signs and lying wonders,* [10]*And with all deceivableness of unrighteousness in them that perish; because they received not the love of the truth, that they might be saved.* [11]*And for this cause God shall send them strong delusion, that they should believe a lie:* [12]*That they all might be damned who believed not the truth, but had pleasure in unrighteousness*" (2 Thessalonians 2:9-12).

Before you take any major decision in your life, pray for divine guidance. I believe this program will guide you to pray well.

PRAYER POINTS

1. Father Lord, arise and guide me into Thy truth, in the name of Jesus.
2. I receive the spirit of revelation to understand spiritual things, in the name of Jesus.
3. Lord Jesus, make Your way plain to me and shed Your light on my ways, in the name of Jesus.
4. Any satanic property in my life, catch fire and burn to ashes, in the name of Jesus.
5. Lord Jesus, reveal to me every secret that will set me free, in the name of Jesus.
6. Blood of Jesus, flow into my foundation and direct my life, in the name of Jesus.
7. Let every secret behind anything happening in my life be revealed, in the name of Jesus.
8. Father Lord, guide me into a place of prosperity, in the name of Jesus.
9. Let the hand of God hold me until I get to my destination, in the name of Jesus.
10. Let the light of God shine on my way and let darkness disappear, in the name of Jesus.
11. Lord Jesus, sprinkle Your blood on my path with the Light of God, in the name of Jesus.
12. Wherever they are waiting to destroy my life, O Lord, help me to escape, in the name of Jesus.
13. Let divine wisdom and knowledge that will promote me overcome me now, in the name of Jesus.

14. Holy Ghost, reveal to me deep secrets that will enlarge my coast, in the name of Jesus.

15. Every demon that is blocking my vision, I cast you out by force, in the name of Jesus.

16. Blood of Jesus, wash away the dirt that is blocking my movements, in the name of Jesus.

17. Anointing to operate with clear spiritual sight, possess me, in the name of Jesus.

18. O Lord, lead me into the fullness of Your grace and glory, in the name of Jesus.

19. I refuse to grope and stumble in this life, in the name of Jesus.

PRAYER FOR CHANGE OF JOB

When Jacob became tired of working for Laban, he desired for a change, and God chose for him a better job. Likewise, if you are tired of a particular job, you can cry to God to choose for you a better job like He did for Jacob. Prayers in this section will be very helpful to you as you trust God for a new job.

> "[38]*This twenty years have I been with thee; thy ewes and thy she goats have not cast their young, and the rams of thy flock have I not eaten.* [39]*That which was torn of beasts I brought not unto thee; I bare the loss of it; of my hand didst thou require it, whether stolen by day, or stolen by night.* [40]*Thus I was; in the day the drought consumed me, and the frost by night; and my sleep departed from mine eyes.* [41]*Thus have I been twenty years in thy house; I served thee fourteen years for thy two daughters, and six years for thy cattle: and thou hast changed my wages ten times.* [42]*Except the God of my father, the God of Abraham, and the fear of Isaac, had been with me, surely thou hadst sent me away now empty. God hath seen mine affliction and the labor of my hands, and rebuked thee yesternight*" (Genesis 31:38-42).

> "[25]*And when he saw that he prevailed not against him, he touched the hollow of his thigh; and the hollow of Jacob's thigh was out of joint, as he wrestled with him.* [26]*And he said, Let me go, for the day breaketh. And he said, I will not let thee go, except thou bless me.* [27]*And he said unto him, What is thy name? And he said, Jacob.* [28]*And he said, Thy name shall be called no more Jacob, but Israel: for as a prince hast thou power with God and with men, and hast prevailed*" (Genesis 32:25-28).

Even when your job is good, you can still pray for a greater one, if you will. Jacob cried out for a change and God changed his name. Peter was a professional fisherman, but when he met Christ, his life changed. Before meeting Christ, he struggled for many years, doing the work he knew how to do. Evidently, he wasn't doing what God wanted him to do in his life until he met Christ.

All may seem well with you and your comfortable job now, but is it really the job God wants you to do on earth? Or you may be going through frustration and desiring God's intervention. Pray fervently and trust God. He is able to change both your life and your job in an instant.

> "[4]*Now when he had left speaking, he said unto Simon, Launch out into the deep, and let down your nets for a draught.* [5]*And Simon answering said unto him, Master, we have toiled all the night, and have taken nothing: nevertheless at thy word I will let down the net.* [6]*And when they had this done, they inclosed a great multitude of fishes: and their net brake.* [7]*And they beckoned unto their partners, which were in the other ship, that they should come and help them. And they came, and filled both the ships, so that they began to sink.* [8]*When Simon Peter saw it, he fell down at Jesus' knees, saying, Depart from me; for I am a sinful man, O Lord.* [9]*For he was astonished, and all that were with him, at the draught of the fishes which they had taken:* [10]*And so was also James, and John, the sons of Zebedee, which were partners with Simon. And Jesus said unto Simon, Fear not; from henceforth thou shalt catch men*" (Luke 5: 4-10).

I pray that you will succeed from today without struggles. With much joy, you will increase and become an employee. As you pray the prayers in this section, Jesus will show you where to cast your nets and you will have a better life in the name of Jesus.

PRAYER POINTS

1. O Lord, arise and utter a Word that will change me forever, in the name of Jesus.
2. Any positive change that will promote me, appear, in the name of Jesus.
3. Any satanic bird that is flying to keep me in one level of life, die, in the name of Jesus.
4. O Lord, arise and take me to another level, in the name of Jesus.
5. Any evil group that is keeping me out of progress, scatter, in the name of Jesus.
6. Any family altar that was assigned to confine me in a particular place, catch fire, in the name of Jesus.
7. Any evil limitation that is placed upon my life, disappear, in the name of Jesus.
8. Father Lord, open up my life to receive Your change, in the name of Jesus.
9. Any evil counselor against great changes in my life, be frustrated, in the name of Jesus.
10. Let the angel of great changes appear for my sake, in the name of Jesus.
11. Any mistake that will bring great a change, appear, in the name of Jesus.
12. O Lord, change my job and make my life better, in the name of Jesus.
13. Any change of job that will affect every area of my life positively, manifest, in the name of Jesus.

14. Blood of Jesus, give me a change of job to Your own glory, in the name of Jesus.

15. Every yoke of evil change in my life, break, in the name of Jesus.

16. Let my enemies make mistakes that will promote me above them, in the name of Jesus.

17. Father Lord, take me into an office that will help me serve You more, in the name of Jesus.

PRAYER TO PREVAIL IN JOB SEEKING

God has created everything everyone needs to succeed in life on earth. Ironically, whatever it is that you are looking for is somewhere starring at you. That's why you need to be born-again, believe and trust God, and prayerfully ask Him to walk you into the path of your purpose on earth. Moses was holding a miraculous rod, yet he never knew it until God revealed it to him.

> "[1]*And Moses answered and said, But, behold, they will not believe me, nor hearken unto my voice: for they will say, The LORD hath not appeared unto thee.* [2]*And the LORD said unto him, What is that in thine hand? And he said, A rod.* [3]*And he said, Cast it on the ground. And he cast it on the ground, and it became a serpent; and Moses fled from before it.* [4]*And the LORD said unto Moses, Put forth thine hand, and take it by the tail. And he put forth his hand, and caught it, and it became a rod in his hand*" (Exodus 4:1-4).

The job of your dreams, which you have sought for many years, may actually be around the corner starring at you. All you need is to pray that God opens your eyes to behold the value of what God has put in your possession.

> "[15]*And the water was spent in the bottle, and she cast the child under one of the shrubs.* [16]*And she went, and sat her down over against him a good way off, as it were a bowshot: for she said, Let me not see the death of the child. And she sat over against him, and lift up her voice, and wept.* [17]*And God heard the voice of the lad; and the angel of God called to Hagar out of heaven, and said unto her, What aileth thee, Hagar? Fear not; for God hath heard the voice of the lad where he is.* [18]*Arise, lift up the lad, and hold him*

in thine hand; for I will make him a great nation. [19]And God opened her eyes, and she saw a well of water; and she went, and filled the bottle with water, and gave the lad drink. [20]And God was with the lad; and he grew, and dwelt in the wilderness, and became an archer" (Genesis 21:15-20).

Pray that God opens your eyes to see the particular job He has destined you to do on earth. Before He created you, God has chosen a particular assignment for you to do for Him on earth. And until you fulfill your assignment, you cannot enjoy true fulfillment of accomplishment. You don't need to waste more time.

PRAYER POINTS

1. O Lord, I want to be employed immediately, in the name of Jesus.

2. Let my job application receive immediate attention by force, in the name of Jesus.

3. O Lord, arise and take me to my right place in life, in the name of Jesus.

4. Father Lord, let me find favor in a good organization and be employed there, in the name of Jesus.

5. Whoever is responsible for employing people must consider me for a good position, in the name of Jesus.

6. O Lord, arise and employ me where I can represent You most, in the name of Jesus.

7. Every enemy of my employment, be disgraced out of your place, in the name of Jesus.

8. O Lord, convince even my enemies to consider me for employment, in the name of Jesus.

9. Any evil personality that is sitting upon my job, be unseated by thunder, in the name of Jesus.

10. Blood of Jesus, speak me into a good job, in the name of Jesus.

11. Holy Ghost fire, burn every evil document against my employment, in the name of Jesus.

12. Father Lord, take me to where the job that will give me peace is, in the name of Jesus.

13. O Lord, destroy any evil report that is working against my job, in the name of Jesus.

14. O Lord, ignore every evil voice that is crying against me and give me a job, in the name of Jesus.

15. Let the job that will end all my poverty and sorrows, appear, in the name of Jesus.

16. Let all evil padlocks that are locking up my jobs break, in the name of Jesus.

17. Any power that is putting my job on hold, you are wicked; die, in the name of Jesus.

18. Heavenly Father, arise and give me a job that will better my life, in the name of Jesus.

19. Any curse that is keeping me out of job, expire, in the name of Jesus.

20. Any inherited covenant that is blocking my way to a better job, break, in the name of Jesus.

21. Let the angels of the living God arise and negotiate for my employment, in the name of Jesus.

22. I command my documents to find favor for a consideration, in the name of Jesus.

PRAYER TO BE SUCCESSFUL IN YOUR JOB

If God is able to give you a job, He is also able to protect your job and make you to be successful doing the job. God did not cease in helping His children to advance until they crossed over the Jordan into the Promised Land. When He starts something, He finishes it.

> "[31]*What shall we then say to these things? If God be for us, who can be against us?* [32] *He that spared not his own Son, but delivered him up for us all, how shall he not with him also freely give us all things?* [33]*Who shall lay anything to the charge of God's elect? It is God that justifieth.* [34]*Who is he that condemneth? It is Christ that died, yea rather, that is risen again, who is even at the right hand of God, who also maketh intercession for us.* [35]*Who shall separate us from the love of Christ? Shall tribulation, or distress, or persecution, or famine, or nakedness, or peril, or sword?* [36]*As it is written, For thy sake we are killed all the day long; we are accounted as sheep for the slaughter.* [37]*Nay, in all these things we are more than conquerors through him that loved us.* [38]*For I am persuaded, that neither death, nor life, nor angels, nor principalities, nor powers, nor things present, nor things to come,* [39]*Nor height, nor depth, nor any other creature, shall be able to separate us from the love of God, which is in Christ Jesus our Lord*" (Romans 8:31-39).

No matter the numbers of your enemies in the place of work, God is able to protect His children and cause them to enjoy the works of their hands. Daniel and the three Hebrew children were never intimidated in their offices. Even when Daniel was thrown into the lion's den, God saved him from wicked conspirators, who then died on his behalf. As you continue being faithful in paying your tithes, living a holy life and praying to God always, you will prevail over all your enemies in your place of work. If you wish to keep your job and enjoy it fully, you must give holiness the place that it deserves and prayerfully trust God to promote you. God will surely help you as you pray the prayers in this book.

However, to some people, sudden promotion often results in sudden failures. Joseph believed God for a job success and he lasted in office serving God and man with God on his side. As a prime minister in Egypt, he was a good administrator, an example of wisdom and foresight in good planning. He was an industrious leader and he was reckoned with success at the end of his life.

PRAYER POINTS

1. O Lord, help me to make a remarkable progress in my place of work, in the name of Jesus.
2. Every problem in my place of work, disappear and die, in the name of Jesus.
3. Blood of Jesus, speak peace for me in my place of work, in the name of Jesus.
4. Father Lord, help me to make great success in this office, in the name of Jesus.
5. Let my input in my job be widely accepted, in the name of Jesus.
6. Any territorial power in my place of work, be destroyed, in the name of Jesus.
7. Every enemy of my job, be exposed and disgraced, in the name of Jesus.
8. I deliver my job from record polluters, in the name of Jesus.
9. O Lord, let my record in my place of work be without blemish, in the name of Jesus.
10. Every agent of devil in my place of work, be frustrated, in the name of Jesus.
11. Every satanic embargo that is placed upon my work, be lifted, in the name of Jesus.
12. Every evil plan that is going on against me in my place of work, fail woefully, in the name of Jesus.
13. I refuse to give up righteousness in my place of work, in the name of Jesus.

14. Blood of Jesus, flow into my place of work and help me to succeed, in the name of Jesus.

15. Every voice of failure in my place of work, be silenced, in the name of Jesus.

16. O Lord, use me to set a standard of success in my place of work, in the name of Jesus.

17. Every Goliath in my place of work, die for my sake, in the name of Jesus.

18. O Lord, make me a pillar of progress in my place of work, in the name of Jesus.

PRAYER FOR SPORTSMEN AND WOMEN

As a sports person, you need both spiritual and physical energy to survive. To excel above others in your field you need God. You have to recognize that without God, you can do nothing. That's why you want to make Him your Lord, so He would lead you into success through your sports career.

> "[6]*Jesus saith unto him, I am the way, the truth, and the life: no man cometh unto the Father, but by me*" (John 14:6).

> "[22]*Look unto me, and be ye saved, all the ends of the earth: for I am God, and there is none else*" (Isaiah 45:22).

Ask for God's grace to live a good life that is pleasing to God. God demands that you use your life, time, money, possession and talents to glorify him. To last long or be the best for a very long time and retire as a great sportsman or woman, you need more grace. The prayers in this program will single you out as the best in every competition. You will be favored to arise above others and take the first position in every game or competitions. The anointing to excel, surpass, outshine and be the best will never depart from you to your last day on earth. If only you would repent and give your life to Christ, these prayers would be very helpful to you.

PRAYER POINTS

1. I receive the grace of God to win in every contest by fire, in the name of Jesus.

2. Let my opponent's gifts and talents be troubled until I get victory, in the name of Jesus.

3. I refuse my opponents to outdo me in the pitch, in the name of Jesus.

4. O Lord, increase my performance and better my tactics, in the name of Jesus.

5. I command my opponents to make mistakes that will favor me, in the name of Jesus.

6. Let my opponents cease from functioning where they are better than I, in the name of Jesus am.

7. Let my opponents receive the anointing of poor performance, in the name of Jesus.

8. I close the door of victory against my opponents in this contest, in the name of Jesus.

9. I command my opponent's progress to slow down till I am declared a winner, in the name Jesus.

10. I fire arrows of incomplete victory at my opponents, in the name of Jesus.

11. Let my opponents be possessed with the anointing of unexplainable errors, in the name of Jesus.

12. You my opponents, until the game is over, I cease your performance, in the name Jesus.

13. I release arrows of confusion against smart and brilliant opponents, in the name of Jesus.

14. I begin to manipulate the talents of my opponents until the game is over, in the name of Jesus.

15. As I enter into the game, let the doors of success be opened to me, in the name of Jesus.

16. If my opponents will score at all, let them score against themselves, in the name of Jesus.

17. You my opponent, you must lack true direction until the game is over, in the name of Jesus.

18. Any power against me in this game, give up the ghost, in the name of Jesus.

19. I receive the power to perform beyond expectations to a level of victory, in the name of Jesus.

20. I cover the eyes of my opponents with veil of confusion until the game is over, in the name of Jesus.

21. All the mistakes that will make me a winner, manifest, in the name of Jesus.

22. Every spirit in me against excellence, die, in the name of Jesus.

23. My enemy's agenda against me in this game must be frustrated, in the name of Jesus.

PRAYER FOR THE TOP EMPLOYMENT

God's plan is for everyone on earth to be gainfully employed. You cannot afford to be idle in a busy world like ours. When God created the earth, he assigned Adam to work in the garden.

> *"[8]And the LORD God planted a garden eastward in Eden; and there he put the man whom he had formed. [9]And out of the ground made the LORD God to grow every tree that is pleasant to the sight, and good for food; the tree of life also in the midst of the garden, and the tree of knowledge of good and evil. [10]And a river went out of Eden to water the garden; and from thence it was parted, and became into four heads. [11]The name of the first is Pison: that is it which compasseth the whole land of Havilah, where there is gold; [12]And the gold of that land is good: there is bdellium and the onyx stone. [13]And the name of the second river is Gihon: the same is it that compasseth the whole land of Ethiopia. [14]And the name of the third river is Hiddekel: that is it which goeth toward the east of Assyria. And the fourth river is Euphrates. [15]And the LORD God took the man, and put him into the garden of Eden to dress it and to keep it"* (Genesis 2:8-15).

God assigned Adam to be in charge of the garden and Eve, his wife, was to help him.

> *"[7]And she said, I pray you, let me glean and gather after the reapers among the sheaves: so she came, and hath continued even from the morning until now, that she tarried a little in the house. [8]Then said Boaz unto Ruth, Hearest thou not, my daughter? Go not to glean in another field, neither go from hence, but abide here fast by my maidens: [9]Let thine eyes be on*

the field that they do reap, and go thou after them: have I not charged the young men that they shall not touch thee? and when thou art athirst, go unto the vessels, and drink of that which the young men have drawn" (Ruth 2:7-9).

"[8]And it fell on a day, that Elisha passed to Shunem, where was a great woman; and she constrained him to eat bread. And so it was, that as oft as he passed by, he turned in thither to eat bread" (2 Kings 4:8).

It is abnormal to stay without a job because it is not God's will. If there is no employment, pray to God to create one for you. It is a sin to be idle without any employment. God, who gave Adam an assignment, will surely help you when you call unto Him.

PRAYER POINTS

1. Every yoke of joblessness in my life, break, in the name of Jesus.

2. O Lord, arise and give me a job that will help me to work for You more, in the name of Jesus.

3. Every spirit of idleness in my life, come out, in the name of Jesus.

4. Any power that has vowed to keep me out of job, I cast you out, in the name of Jesus.

5. Holy Ghost fire, burn every delay of getting a good job, in the name of Jesus.

6. Father Lord, put people that will employ me in right positions, in the name of Jesus.

7. Any evil personality that has vowed to sit upon my job, be unseated, in the name of Jesus.

8. Wherever my C.V. reaches for a job, O Lord, move the authority to employ me, in the name of Jesus.

9. Blood of Jesus, flow into every office and negotiate my employment, in the name of Jesus.

10. Father Lord, make a way for me where there is no way, in the name of Jesus.

11. Any evil altar of my parents' house that is sitting upon my employment, catch fire, in the name of Jesus.

12. Any evil utterance against my employment, expire, in the name of Jesus.

13. O Lord, grant me favor to be employed in a right place, in the name of Jesus.

14. Every enemy of my employment, be disgraced, in the name of Jesus.

15. O Lord, help me to perform excellently well in any job interview, in the name of Jesus.

16. Let me be preferred above other job seekers, in the name of Jesus.

17. Any strongman that is working hard to keep me out of job, die, in the name of Jesus.

18. Any wall of Jericho that is standing between my job and I, collapse, in the name of Jesus.

19. Any evil gang up against my job, scatter, in the name of Jesus.

20. O Lord, give me a job by Your mercy, in the name of Jesus.

21. Any evil condition that is attached to my job, I reject you, in the name of Jesus.

22. O Lord, give me a job without further delay, in the name of Jesus.

23. O Lord, remove the peace of those who are supposed to give me a job until they do so, in the name of Jesus.

24. Father Lord, arise and guide me to get a good job, in the name of Jesus.

PRAYER FOR WISDOM TO BECOME SELF-EMPLOYED

There are millions of job seekers all over the world today. The number of job seekers in the global labor market is massive. If nothing is done urgently, we may head into such global problems that are able to frustrate governments and the world populace. We need prayers that can help more people become self-employed. Billions of jobs that can change destinies of the world's populace are in the hands of God. He is the one who has created jobs for all of us before He created us.

> "[7]*And these things give in charge, that they may be blameless.* [8]*But if any provide not for his own, and especially for those of his own house, he hath denied the faith, and is worse than an infidel*" (1 Timothy 5:7-8).

No individual, especially men, would be blameless when he fails to provide for himself and his household. If the government has failed to provide any job for you, you cannot afford to fail yourself and your own family also. It is a disgrace for anyone to roam the streets or stay idle without anything to do. When your parents or the government cannot do anything, then you have to rise up and do something for yourself. It is disheartening to go into crimes because you lack a job to do.

I read in a Nigerian newspaper, Guardian Newspaper - 12/04/1999, how Bill Gates discovered his destiny and dropped every other thing he was doing to start building computer in his garage.

The paper wrote, Gates, 34 year's old, holds over one billion shares in the Seattle (United States) based software giant each of which is worth $93. He also has shareholdings in several other companies, including 89 billion invested in satellite ventures. The daily telegraph reports that having made about $4,566,000 for every hour of the past year, and with his wealth growing at 61 percent compound yearly rate it has enjoyed so far, he will hit the #1,000,000,000,000 mark in 2004. The paper also said, Gate's current wealth exceeded the economic output of all but 18 wealthiest nations. Indeed, if his wealth continues to snow ball, it should overtake Britain gross national product in 2015.

Also, on Thursday August 5, 2010, I picked up Daily Mail newspaper at Heathrow airport United Kingdom, and on the 7th page I saw a title, 'Billionaires give half their fortune to charities.' Among them was Bill Gates. He was a co-founder of Microsoft and he remains the biggest shareholder with a net worth of £33 billion. With his wife Melinda, 54, he set up the Bill and Melinda Gates foundation in 2000, which remains one of the largest aid organizations in the world, and has donated more than £17 billion to charities.

Another person is Barron Hilton, one of the sons of Conrad Hilton, who started the Hilton Hotel chain. He has a fortune estimated at £1.6 billion and wanted to leave 79 percent of it to a charitable trust. Ted, who is the founder of CNN, worth about £1.1 billion. He supports UN causes. Warren Buffett was the third richest man in the world. He slipped down the rankings as he gave money away. He made £30 billion fortune through investments with his company Berkshire Hathaway. In 2006, the 79 year-old vowed to donate 90 percent of his wealth to charity.

Michael Bloomberg, financial news tycoon with a £12 billion fortune, who is serving his third term as mayor of New York. Mr. Bloomberg, 68, once said, *"I have always said that the best financial planning ends with bouncing the cheque to the undertaker."* George Lucas, who ranks among the most successful filmmakers of all time, has personal fortune of around £2 billion. The star wars director, 66, has received a string of Academy Awards. Star wars made over $400 million on its first run alone. Paul Allen, unmarried with no children, has £8.7 billion fortune for co-founding Microsoft.

He has already given away $1 billion through foundations he has created.

Diane von Furstenberg, a 63-year-old designer and her TV Mogul husband, Barry Diller, 68, have a fortune of more than £1 billion J. Boon Pickens, 82, of capital management is worth about £2 billion. David Rockefeller worth £2 billion. In 2008, Rockefeller gave $100 million to Harvard. This unprecedented commitment was brokered by Microsoft founder Bill Gates and investor Warren Buffet over a series of intimate dinners.

Gates, whose $53 billion fortune placed him second on the list of worlds' richest people, and Buffett, who ranked third, initiated these pledges. They wanted to persuade hundreds of US billionaires to give away most of their fortune during their life time or after their death and to publicly state their intentions. So far, 50 billionaires have signed up.

Dorcas Erskine, from Charity Action Aid, said, *"The donors were leading by examples. It is not just about the money but also the experience and talent that these individuals bring to the table."* And Caroline Preston, from the New York based chronicle of philanthropy, added, *"Bill Gates and warren sufficiently have been moved by other philanthropy and Gates is directing all of his time towards it now."*

Sarah's maid, Hagar, lost her job, house and protection. She cast her only child under one of the shrubs in the wilderness of Beersheba. She handed her only child to death and lost every hope in life. When the rejected child; an illegitimate son of Abraham from a bondwoman, began to cry, God heard his voice. When you cry to God for wisdom on what to do, He is able to open your eyes to discover businesses that can make you a millionaire or one of the richest people in your generation.

> *"[17]And God heard the voice of the lad; and the angel of God called to Hagar out of heaven, and said unto her, What aileth thee, Hagar? fear not; for God hath heard the voice of the lad where he is"* (Genesis 21:17).

There are many invisible business opportunities in the world. Through prayers, the Lord can open your spiritual eyes that are blind to discover a business that can make you great. Ironically, there are many Bill Gates in the world today, who are jobless and penniless. But as you continue praying these prayers, the Lord can open your eyes, empower you and make you the Warren Buffett of your time.

Peter was a professional; a veteran fisherman, who recorded much failures. He told Jesus, *"Master, we have toiled all the nigh, and have taken nothing"*. There are many people like Peter in the world today. They are almost at the point of giving up. They dread the thought of getting older and older, without achieving anything. The only thing such people are good at is being confused and disappointed, even when they are so intelligent and brilliant.

In the case of Peter, a fresh breathe of life came his way the day he decided to give every other thing up in order to follow Jesus. He handed his life to the Lord and became a disciple. If you desire power to create millions of jobs, feed nations and leave your wealth for millions of less privileged families, Jesus is calling on you to leave every other thing behind and follow Him. Then all things you need would be given back to you.

> *"[4]Now when he had left speaking, he said unto Simon, Launch out into the deep, and let down your nets for a draught. [5]And Simon answering said unto him, Master, we have toiled all the night, and have taken nothing: nevertheless at thy word I will let down the net. [6]And when they had this done, they inclosed a great multitude of fishes: and their net brake. [7]And they beckoned unto their partners, which were in the other ship, that they should come and help them. And they came, and filled both the ships, so that they began to sink"* (Luke 5:4-7).

> *"[17]Elias was a man subject to like passions as we are, and he prayed earnestly that it might not rain: and it rained not on the earth by the space of three years*

and six months. [18]*And he prayed again, and the heaven gave rain, and the earth brought forth her fruit"* (James 5:17-18).

Michael Bloomberg was an ordinary man but God made him the financial news tycoon with a £12 billion fortune. Diara von Furstenberg was an ordinary woman. But the Lord made her to discover her talent as a designer. She was best known for her wrap dress whilst she approved shows like the Simpson's when working at Fox Television. Melinda, the wife of Bill Gates and her husband set up the Melinda Gates foundation, which is one of the largest aid organizations in the world. Melinda Gates foundation has donated more than £17 billion to charity and various causes. Wouldn't it be a disgrace to live and die without any legacy or personal accomplishment that can touch other people's lives?

These forty American billionaires are rebuke to all the rich people in other countries, especially to African, in general, and Nigeria, in particular. It is also a challenge to world leaders to come up with divinely motivated policies that can employ and empower the people they lead. Ask the Lord to help you discover a talent or gift within you. You need to pray and command this talent or gift to manifest. Life will no longer be a struggle when you discover yourself. Pray that the seed within you germinates and bears fruits. When you discover your destiny and God's purpose for your life, you will excel above others in any field.

A discovered destiny helps a person to be distinguished and outstanding. It is time to stop seeing yourself as nobody. You are a divine asset. When the talent or gift inside you radiates, the whole world will notice it. Then you cannot hide any longer but rise and shine in your field of endeavor. People, who have discovered their destinies, do exceptional things. They become the best among the best and remain unsurpassed until death and ever after.

PRAYER POINTS

1. Father Lord, empower me to discover my destiny, in the name of Jesus.

2. Lord Jesus, give me a divine motivated vision that will glorify Your name, in the name of Jesus.

3. Let the power to focus towards a divine direction possess me, in the name of Jesus.

4. I command every demonic distraction in my life to depart, in the name of Jesus.

5. O Lord, help me to focus towards Your purpose for my life, in the name of Jesus.

6. Blood of Jesus, help me not to be shortsighted, in the name of Jesus.

7. Let the power to communicate my vision to genuine people possess me, in the name of Jesus.

8. O Lord, commission people who would be involved in my vision, in the name of Jesus.

9. I receive power to meet genuine people in life, in the name of Jesus.

10. O Lord, compel genuine people to get involved in my vision, in the name of Jesus.

11. Father Lord, arise and globalize my vision, in the name of Jesus.

12. Let people who will assist me buy into my vision, in the name of Jesus.

13. Let the people of the world welcome my vision with all their hearts, in the name of Jesus.

14. Let the presence of God appear fully in my vision, in the name of Jesus.

15. Lord Jesus, raise genuine people to be excited with my vision, in the name of Jesus.

16. Father Lord, build a divinely motivated team around me, in the name of Jesus.

17. Let people that will bring the vision of my life to light appear, in the name of Jesus.

18. O Lord, let the people You bring begin to contribute towards my vision, in the name of Jesus.

19. Let people in my team be rightly assigned, in the name of Jesus.

20. Father Lord, frustrate the devil and his agents, in the name of Jesus.

21. I command vision builders to joyfully manifest to work with me, in the name of Jesus.

22. Let the unity that exists between the Godhead control my team, in the name of Jesus.

23. Let my vision be the purpose for the team's existence, in the name of Jesus.

24. O Lord, develop the wisdom and knowledge of each team member on daily basis, in the name of Jesus.

25. Let heaven stir up each team member unto right actions, in the name of Jesus.

26. Let heavenly forces enter into each team member by force, in the name of Jesus.

27. O Lord, increase the faith of each team member to Your glory, in the name of Jesus.

28. Let the faith of every team member be in Christ Jesus, in the name of Jesus.

29. Father Lord, develop the thought life and prayer life of every team member, in the name of Jesus.

30. Let divine strategy be released to accomplish every vision, in the name of Jesus.

31. I command divine strength to fall on all members, in the name of Jesus.

32. Let every member be gifted to specialize on right areas, in the name of Jesus.

33. O Lord, raise great champions with unity in every department, in the name of Jesus.

34. Let my team members become friends and value each other, in the name of Jesus.

35. Blood of Jesus, flow into every team member and create genuine commitment, in the name of Jesus.

36. Let forces from heaven aid every team member, in the name of Jesus.

37. I command unity, love and the nine fruits of the Spirit to reign, in the name of Jesus.

38. Let there be holy intentions, commitments and accomplishments to the glory of God, in the name of Jesus.

39. O Lord, provide for every vision, in the name of Jesus.

40. O Lord, help us to view what we achieved yesterday as too little for today, in the name of Jesus.

41. O Lord, empower me to make things happen in my generation, in the name of Jesus.

42. Father Lord, give me a vision that will destroy my frustrations, in the name of Jesus.

43. O Lord, give me a job and empower me to overcome discouragement, in the name of Jesus.

44. I command every seed inside me to germinate by force, in the name of Jesus.

45. Let my gift and talent escape from every evil confinement by force, in the name of Jesus.

46. I command the tree of my destiny to grow and bear fruits that will be seen globally, in the name of Jesus.

47. Blood of Jesus, sharpen my creative mind and spread my ideas globally, in the name of Jesus.

48. Any power that wants my seed to die young, be destroyed, in the name of Jesus.

49. Let the power of heaven force every enemy of my vision to die, in the name of Jesus.

50. I break and loose myself from every satanic bondage, in the name of Jesus.

51. Father Lord, show me where to cast my nets on earth, in the name of Jesus.

PRAYER TO BE GAINFULLY EMPLOYED

One of the worst things that can happen to any person, especially adults, is to be out of job and penniless. It is equally catastrophic for any nation not to be able to provide jobs for its citizens or citizens not to provide jobs for themselves.

> *"[8]But if any provide not for his own, and especially for those of his own house, he hath denied the faith, and is worse than an infidel"* (1 Timothy 5:8).

> *"[10]For even when we were with you, this we commanded you, that if any would not work, neither should he eat. [11]For we hear that there are some which walk among you disorderly, working not at all, but are busybodies"* (2 Thessalonica 3:10-11).

What most people fail to understand is that God created every individual with a particular gift, talent and an assignment to accomplish on earth. No matter where you are or what you have, there is a job waiting for you. I pray that God gives you the grace of gainful employment. The prayers here are designed to guide you as you pray for a good job that can help you fulfill your destiny. Break and lose yourself from the captivity of unemployment. It is well with you in the name of our Lord Jesus.

PRAYER POINTS

1. Any power that has vowed to keep me out of job, die, in the name of Jesus.

2. I refuse to stay longer than necessary in the labor market, in the name of Jesus.

3. Father Lord, give me a job that will allow me to serve You more, in the name of Jesus.

4. I break and loose myself from rejections, in the name of Jesus.

5. Every mark of hatred in my life, die, in the name of Jesus.

6. Let the blood of Jesus empower me to get a good job, in the name of Jesus.

7. Every inherited poverty that is keeping me out of job, break, in the name of Jesus.

8. Blood of Jesus, flow into my foundation and deliver me, in the name of Jesus.

9. I move from the bondage of unemployment to a profitable employment, in the name of Jesus.

10. Let the strongman keeping me out of job die by fire, in the name of Jesus.

11. I cancel all enchantments and curses behind my employment, in the name of Jesus.

12. Any evil utterance that is made against my getting divinely appointed job, expire, in the name of Jesus.

13. Every stubborn oppressor that is preventing me from getting a job, die by force, in the name of Jesus.

14. O Lord, take me to the office which You have prepared for me, in the name of Jesus.

15. Any evil personality that is sitting upon my job, be unseated by death, in the name of Jesus.

16. Any wall of Jericho that is standing against my job, collapse, in the name of Jesus.

17. Every evil decree made against my employment, I render you useless, in the name of Jesus.

18. Any power that is in agreement with my joblessness, scatter, in the name of Jesus.

19. I overthrow every evil judgment that is directed at me, in the name of Jesus.

20. I stand against any power that is rising to stop me from getting a job, in the name of Jesus.

21. O Lord, influence high authorities to give me a job without delay, in the name of Jesus.

PRAYER TO GET A BETTER JOB

It is not bad to pray for a better job even you have one already. You may not need to resign from where you are working before moving into another job. There is no need for a rush. If you must settle for a better job, you can remain faithful at your work place in the meantime as you continue praying for the right job at a time.

> *"[38]This twenty years have I been with thee; thy ewes and thy she goats have not cast their young, and the rams of thy flock have I not eaten. [39]That which was torn of beasts I brought not unto thee; I bare the loss of it; of my hand didst thou require it, whether stolen by day, or stolen by night. [40]Thus I was; in the day the drought consumed me, and the frost by night; and my sleep departed from mine eyes. [41]Thus have I been twenty years in thy house; I served thee fourteen years for thy two daughters, and six years for thy cattle: and thou hast changed my wages ten times"* (Genesis 31:38-41).

When Jacob discovered that his job did not favor him, he prayed and God asked him to leave. Because God was involved in his leaving, He defended him and changed his name. When you pray, God is able to help you get a better job.

> *"[24]And Jacob was left alone; and there wrestled a man with him until the breaking of the day. [25]And when he saw that he prevailed not against him, he touched the hollow of his thigh; and the hollow of Jacob's thigh was out of joint, as he wrestled with him. [26]And he said, Let me go, for the day breaketh. And he said, I will not let thee go, except thou bless me. [27]And he said unto him, What is thy name? And he said, Jacob. [28]And he said, Thy name shall be*

> *called no more Jacob, but Israel: for as a prince hast thou power with God and with men, and hast prevailed"* (Genesis 32:24-28).

Pray for a job that will give you the opportunity to please God, provide for yourself, help others and sponsor God's work. You need a job that can give you peace and satisfaction. There is nothing impossible for God to do for you.

PRAYER POINTS

1. Father Lord, I pray for a better job that will glorify You, in the name of Jesus.
2. Any power that is withstanding better jobs for me, die, in the name of Jesus.
3. O Lord, arise and cause a new thing to take place in my life, in the name of Jesus.
4. Let the forces of darkness that are keeping me out of new jobs scatter, in the name of Jesus.
5. Blood of Jesus, favor me with a new job, in the name of Jesus.
6. Any satanic delay to get a new and better job, disappear, in the name of Jesus.
7. Holy Ghost fire, burn every enemy a better job for me, in the name of Jesus.
8. O Lord, remove or change all agents that are hindering my new job, in the name of Jesus.
9. Lord Jesus, bring me into favor before people that will give me better jobs, in the name of Jesus.
10. Spirit of excellence for a new and better job, possess me, in the name of Jesus.
11. Let divine substitute take place for a better employment to come, in the name of Jesus.
12. Lord Jesus, favor me exceedingly to get a new and better job, in the name of Jesus.
13. Father Lord, release Your angels to locate a better job for me, in the name of Jesus.

14. Every enemy of new and better jobs for me, resign or go on transfer, in the name of Jesus.

15. Every change that will fetch a new and better job for me, manifest, in the name of Jesus.

16. O Lord, smoothen my way to secure a better job, in the name of Jesus.

17. Any opposition that has built up against my new job, scatter in shame, in the name of Jesus.

18. Power to excel and satisfy the authorities for a better job, possess me, in the name of Jesus.

19. Any spiritual or physical blockage of a better job for me, die, in the name of Jesus.

20. I receive a letter of employment for a better job, in the name of Jesus.

PRAYER BEFORE MOVING INTO A NEW PLACE

Many people carry their past into their future. Wherever they go, they carry their evil past with them, and mix it up with their present lives. You cannot afford to continue living in your past. Pray that God gives you the strength to forget your evil past.

> "[3]*And Samuel spake unto all the house of Israel, saying, If ye do return unto the LORD with all your hearts, then put away the strange gods and Ashtaroth from among you, and prepare your hearts unto the LORD, and serve him only: and he will deliver you out of the hand of the Philistines.* [4]*Then the children of Israel did put away Baalim and Ashtaroth, and served the LORD only*" (1 Samuel 7:3-4).

It is very important to always deal with your past or cleanse your foundation before stepping into the present and the future. This is a healthy thing to do always.

> "[29]*Or else how can one enter into a strong man's house, and spoil his goods, except he first bind the strong man? and then he will spoil his house*" (Matthew 12:29).

> "[6]*This is the generation of them that seek him that seek thy face, O Jacob. Selah.* [7]*Lift up your heads, O ye gates; and be ye lift up, ye everlasting doors; and the King of glory shall come in.* [9]*Lift up your heads, O ye gates; even lift them up, ye everlasting doors; and the King of glory shall come in*" (Psalms 24:6-7, 9).

You need to deal with resident powers of darkness that occupy new places you want to move into. When you fail to prayerfully discharge all evil powers following you, they will join forces with the ones in the new place you are moving into to fight you. When you enter into a new place without casting resident demons out, they may live with you in that house or even make your life very miserable.

> "[30]*Thou shalt betroth a wife, and another man shall lie with her: thou shalt build an house, and thou shalt not dwell therein: thou shalt plant a vineyard, and shalt not gather the grapes thereof*" (Deuteronomy 28:30).

Every environment has its altar that must be destroyed so that God's altar can be raised.

PRAYER POINTS

1. Any power that is blocking my way, I clear you by force, in the name of Jesus.

2. Any evil power that has vowed to keep me at a particular level in life, die, in the name of Jesus.

3. O God, release my divine destiny from satanic detention, in the name of Jesus.

4. Any evil program that is going on against my life, be terminated, in the name of Jesus.

5. I refuse to surrender to my enemies' wishes no matter the pressures, in the name of Jesus.

6. Any power that is increasing my problems, die in shame, in the name of Jesus.

7. Any evil chain that I inherited from my parents, break, in the name of Jesus.

8. Any evil delay on my way to my place of destiny, disappear by force, in the name of Jesus.

9. Any useless program that is designed to keep me away from God's will, die, in the name of Jesus.

10. O Lord, take me to a new place and enlarge my coast, in the name of Jesus.

11. Any power that is contending with my progress, die and be buried, in the name of Jesus.

12. I command every form of darkness on my way to disappear, in the name of Jesus.

13. I receive the anointing of God to move towards a new ground, in the name of Jesus.

14. Any resident evil force that is blocking my way, scatter and die, in the name of Jesus.

15. Any power that is keeping me behind schedule, be wasted, in the name of Jesus.

16. Any evil spy that is monitoring my movement, die, in the name of Jesus.

17. I command destiny killers to be wasted, in the name of Jesus.

18. O Lord, arise and take me to a place in life, in the name of Jesus.

19. Any power that is claiming to be the owner of my promised land, die, in the name of Jesus.

20. Any altar of darkness in my promised land, catch fire, burn to ashes, in the name of Jesus.

21. Any witch or wizard that has vowed to die instead of seeing me succeed, be it according to your word, in the name of Jesus.

22. Let that backbone standing against my movement break, in the name of Jesus.

23. I withdraw all my enemies' helpers by force, in the name of Jesus.

24. Any satanic arrow that has been fired to halt my settlement, backfire, in the name of Jesus.

25. Any desert spirit that has vowed to stop me, die, in the name of Jesus.

26. Any witchcraft decision that is made against my life, be wiped out, in the name of Jesus.

27. Any evil mark that is pulling me down, dry up, in the name of Jesus.

28. Every chain of backwardness that is holding me down, break, in the name of Jesus.

29. Any power that has vowed to wound me, die by force, in the name of Jesus.

30. Any Delilah or Jezebel on my way, be wasted, in the name of Jesus.

31. Any agent of death that is assigned to kill me, go and kill your sender, in the name of Jesus.

32. O Lord, take me into my land of promise, in the name of Jesus.

33. You, Goliath that is living in my promise land, die, in the name of Jesus.

34. Let all invisible dark powers living in my place depart by force, in the name of Jesus.

35. Every evil gang-up, spiritual or physical, scatter, in the name of Jesus.

36. Any battle that is going on against me in this place, known or unknown, let it end to my favor, in the name of Jesus.

37. Let all unfriendly friends be exposed and disgraced, in the name of Jesus.

38. O Lord, arise and prosper me in this new land, in the name of Jesus.

39. Lord Jesus, give me new and sincere friends in this land, in the name of Jesus.

40. Father Lord, favor me exceedingly in this new place, in the name of Jesus.

PRAYER TO EXCEL ABOVE YOUR MASTERS

If there is no particular area in your life where you perform far better than others, then you may need to pray seriously the prayers in this program. God did not create anybody to be average. Every person is unique. This uniqueness distinguishes you.

> "[13]*And the LORD shall make thee the head, and not the tail; and thou shalt be above only, and thou shalt not be beneath; if that thou hearken unto the commandments of the LORD thy God, which I command thee this day, to observe and to do them"* (Deuteronomy 28:13).

> "[1]*It pleased Darius to set over the kingdom an hundred and twenty princes, which should be over the whole kingdom;* [2]*And over these three presidents; of whom Daniel was first: that the princes might give accounts unto them, and the king should have no damage.* [3]*Then this Daniel was preferred above the presidents and princes, because an excellent spirit was in him; and the king thought to set him over the whole realm"* (Daniel 6:1-3).

As you pray through this program, God will help you to discover your area of specialization and excellence. This is where you will have the capacity to rise, surpass your equals and be distinguished from the rest. To excel means to be first-rated. It does not necessarily mean that you should be a jack of all trade or excel in every profession. You need to discover your place on earth, where you would be distinguished in your service to God and humanity.

PRAYER POINTS

1. Anointing for excellence, possess me now, in the name of Jesus.

2. O Lord, help me to rise and be distinguished by fire, in the name of Jesus.

3. I rise and surpass others in my area of gifting, in the name of Jesus.

4. Let the grace of God to shine possess me now, in the name of Jesus.

5. Father Lord, make me best of the best among the rest, in the name of Jesus.

6. I walk into the front row in the areas of my talent, in the name of Jesus.

7. Grace of God to be outstanding in the midst of others, possess me, in the name of Jesus.

8. O Lord, bless me by Your power, in the name of Jesus.

9. O Lord, give me exceptional wisdom and knowledge now, in the name of Jesus.

10. You my life, receive the blessing of excellence, in the name of Jesus.

11. I put on divine garment to be exceptionally different from others, in the name of Jesus.

12. O Lord, make me more valuable than my competitors, in the name of Jesus.

13. Anointing for perfection, manifest in my life today, in the name of Jesus.

14. O Lord, empower me to develop to the highest level according to Your will, in the name of Jesus.

15. Let my destiny receive God's grace to be perfect, in the name of Jesus.

16. Power to excel in any competition in life, possess me, in the name of Jesus.

17. Any evil personality that has vowed to pull me down, be disgraced, in the name of Jesus.

18. Any evil sacrifice offered to bring me down, expire, in the name of Jesus.

19. Let the sacrifice of Jesus mold me to be like Him, in the name of Jesus.

20. Let my excellence be preferred above other excellences, in the name of Jesus.

21. Any problem that was assigned to slow me down, die, in the name of Jesus.

22. God's project in my life will be completed with speed, in the name of Jesus.

PRAYER TO EXCEL IN JOB INTERVIEW

As a child of God, you need to excel in everything you do on earth. You cannot afford to fail any job interview when it is the will of your Father in heaven to secure such jobs. Always remember to commit all your ways in the hands of the Almighty, and He knows how to cause everything you do to prosper.

> "[13]*And the LORD shall make thee the head, and not the tail; and thou shalt be above only, and thou shalt not be beneath; if that thou hearken unto the commandments of the LORD thy God, which I command thee this day, to observe and to do them*" (Deuteronomy 28:13).

> "[7]*When a man's ways please the LORD, he maketh even his enemies to be at peace with him*" (Proverbs 16:7).

If any job belongs to you, you will perform excellently well when you attend the interview. Your appearance before the people that will interview you will be like the appearance of an angel. As you pray, God is able to increase your wisdom to perform far above others.

> "[1]*It pleased Darius to set over the kingdom an hundred and twenty princes, which should be over the whole kingdom;* [2]*And over these three presidents; of whom Daniel was first: that the princes might give accounts unto them, and the king should have no damage.* [3]*Then this Daniel was preferred above the presidents and princes, because an excellent spirit was in him; and the king thought to set him over the whole realm*" (Daniel 6:1-3).

"[15]Now when the turn of Esther, the daughter of Abihail the uncle of Mordecai, who had taken her for his daughter, was come to go in unto the king, she required nothing but what Hegai the king's chamberlain, the keeper of the women, appointed. And Esther obtained favor in the sight of all them that looked upon her. [16]So Esther was taken unto king Ahasuerus into his house royal in the tenth month, which is the month Tebeth, in the seventh year of his reign. [17]And the king loved Esther above all the women, and she obtained grace and favor in his sight more than all the virgins; so that he set the royal crown upon her head, and made her queen instead of Vashti" (Esther 2:15-17).

These prayers will guild you to trust God to make you exceptional among many others. You will be preferred above others in your interview in the name of Jesus. God will help you to find favor before your interviewers in the name of Jesus. Your performance will be recognized and you will be favored exceedingly with unmerited favors no matter what devil does, in the name of Jesus.

PRAYER POINTS

1. Anointing to perform better than others, possess me, in the name of Jesus.

2. O Lord, represent me in the eyes of the panel and make me the best, in the name of Jesus.

3. I cast out from my life any spirit of rejection and hatred, in the name of Jesus.

4. O Lord, give me an excellent spirit to be preferred above others, in the name of Jesus.

5. Let my brain process all answers to every question, in the name of Jesus.

6. Holy Ghost fire, burn every enemy of my life in this interview, in the name of Jesus.

7. Blood of Jesus, empower me to get this job, in the name of Jesus.

8. I silence every evil voice that is speaking against me in this interview, in the name of Jesus.

9. Any weapon that has been deployed to disqualify me in this interview, I destroy you, in the name of Jesus.

10. Lord Jesus, arise and perfect Your plans in my life, in the name of Jesus.

11. Every satanic agenda against my appearance, be frustrated, in the name of Jesus.

12. O Lord, empower me to give correct answers to every question, in the name of Jesus.

13. Any chain of failure that is withholding me in this program, break, in the name of Jesus.

14. I break and loose myself from the spirit of failure, in the name of Jesus.

15. Power of God, empower me to satisfy my interviewers beyond their requirements, in the name of Jesus.

16. I receive divine boldness to give more than is required in this interview, in the name of Jesus.

17. O Lord, let my appearance convince the panel to choose me as their best, in the name of Jesus.

18. Every enemy of my performance through this interview, be frustrated to my favor, in the name of Jesus.

19. Anointing for first class position, possess me, in the name of Jesus.

20. I withdraw myself from failures and defeat, in the name of Jesus.

21. Heavenly Father, open Your heaven and favor me in this interview, in the name of Jesus.

22. Any strongman that is standing against me in this interview, die, in the name of Jesus.

23. O Lord, let the result of this interview favor me, in the name of Jesus.

PRAYER TO FORCE YOUR ENEMIES OUT OF YOUR LIFE

One of the most glaring challenges on earth is that many people do not know how to differentiate their enemies from true friends. As a result, many people have died in the hands of their best friends, who turned around to betray them.

> "[3]*And they said unto him, Thus saith Hezekiah, This day is a day of trouble, and of rebuke, and of blasphemy: for the children are come to the birth, and there is not strength to bring forth*" (Isaiah 37:3).

> "[8]*And Cain talked with Abel his brother: and it came to pass, when they were in the field, that Cain rose up against Abel his brother, and slew him*" (Genesis 4:8).

> "[19]*And she made him sleep upon her knees; and she called for a man, and she caused him to shave off the seven locks of his head; and she began to afflict him, and his strength went from him.* [20]*And she said, The Philistines be upon thee, Samson. And he awoke out of his sleep, and said, I will go out as at other times before, and shake myself. And he wist not that the LORD was departed from him.* [21]*But the Philistines took him, and put out his eyes, and brought him down to Gaza, and bound him with fetters of brass; and he did grind in the prison house*" (Judges 16:19-21).

Your enemies plant evil seeds in your life while you sleep. They change good things coming towards you to evil. Evil powers that trade with people's destinies are enemies.

Enemies feed people in their dreams with evil foods and drinks. They take innocent people into captivities without mercy and deny them their rights and entitlements. Enemies are very antagonistic. You need to discover who your enemies are, and then fight or avoid them forever. This is one of the best discoveries on earth. Otherwise, it would be easy to fall into the hand of your enemy.

PRAYER POINTS

1. I command every unrepentant enemy to be forced out of their places of rest, in the name of Jesus.

2. I withdraw every support my enemies are receiving to attack me, in the name of Jesus.

3. Blood of Jesus, overrun my enemies with sorrows, in the name of Jesus.

4. I command my enemies to make mistakes that will frustrate them, in the name of Jesus.

5. Any evil brain that is thinking against my life, scatter by thunder, in the name of Jesus.

6. Let the activities of my enemies begin to work against them, in the name of Jesus.

7. I command the earth to rise against every enemy of my destiny, in the name of Jesus.

8. Every organized enemy of my life, be disorganized by fire, in the name of Jesus.

9. O Lord, arise and remove the comfort of the wicked, in the name of Jesus.

10. Every satanic network that is empowering my enemies, scatter, in the name of Jesus.

11. Every pit my enemies have dug for me, swallow them now, in the name of Jesus.

12. Let the problems of my enemies be multiplied, in the name of Jesus.

13. I command darkness to cover enemies of my peace, in the name of Jesus.

14. I fire arrows of poverty and lack at my enemies, in the name of Jesus.

15. I command the problems of my enemies to increase by force, in the name of Jesus.

16. Every agent of defeat and failures, arrest my enemies now, in the name of Jesus.

17. Let satanic weapons locate my enemies and take them captives, in the name of Jesus.

18. Let the backbone of my enemies break to pieces, in the name of Jesus.

19. Every instrument of peace provided for my enemies, be withdrawn, in the name of Jesus.

20. I increase oppressors for my enemies by force, in the name of Jesus.

PRAYER TO FORCE YOUR ENEMIES TO BOW

There are prayers that can force enemies to bow. You need to start praying such prayers. Once you start praying such prayers, no enemy can resist or withstand your utterances.

> "[31]*Then said Jesus to those Jews which believed on him, If ye continue in my word, then are ye my disciples indeed;* [32]*And ye shall know the truth, and the truth shall make you free.* [36]*If the Son therefore shall make you free, ye shall be free indeed"* (John 8:31-32, 36).

If you are truly born-again and you know your rights as a disciple of Christ indeed, no power of darkness can remain consistent in your life. Prayers that will deliver you are in this book and if you put them into practice, all your enemies will be forced to bow.

> "[25]*But while men slept, his enemy came and sowed tares among the wheat, and went his way.* [26]*But when the blade was sprung up, and brought forth fruit, then appeared the tares also"* (Matthew 13:25-26).

> "[3]*And they said unto him, Thus saith Hezekiah, This day is a day of trouble, and of rebuke, and of blasphemy: for the children are come to the birth, and there is not strength to bring forth"* (Isaiah 37:3).

> "[6]*And the angels which kept not their first estate, but left their own habitation, he hath reserved in everlasting chains under darkness unto the judgment of the great day.* [7]*Even as Sodom and Gomorrha, and the cities about them in like manner, giving themselves over to fornication, and going*

after strange flesh, are set forth for an example, suffering the vengeance of eternal fire. [8]Likewise also these filthy dreamers defile the flesh, despise dominion, and speak evil of dignities" (Jude 1:6-8).

Evil powers that constantly plant evil into your life are your enemies. These powers ruin good things coming your way. Evil powers trade and make gains with people's destinies. They feed you in your dreams to reduce your capacity.

"[16]And it came to pass, as we went to prayer, a certain damsel possessed with a spirit of divination met us, which brought her masters much gain by soothsaying: [17]The same followed Paul and us, and cried, saying, These men are the servants of the most high God, which shew unto us the way of salvation. [18]And this did she many days. But Paul, being grieved, turned and said to the spirit, I command thee in the name of Jesus Christ to come out of her. And he came out the same hour. [19]And when her masters saw that the hope of their gains was gone, they caught Paul and Silas, and drew them into the marketplace unto the rulers" (Acts 16:16-19).

These powers deny people of their rights, benefits and entitlements, and keep them in bondage. They also arrest people's progresses and bury their destinies. But they will not see you because the blood of Jesus covers you, Amen.

"[17]They did cry there, Pharaoh king of Egypt is but a noise; he hath passed the time appointed" (Jeremiah 46:17).

"[11]And it came to pass the day after, that he went into a city called Nain; and many of his disciples went with him, and much people. [12]Now when he came nigh to the gate of the city, behold, there was a dead man carried out, the only son of his mother, and she was a widow: and much people of the city was with her. [13]And when the Lord saw her, he had compassion on her, and said unto her, Weep not. [14]And he came and touched the bier: and they that

bare him stood still. And he said, Young man, I say unto thee, Arise. [15]*And he that was dead sat up, and began to speak. And he delivered him to his mother.* [16]*And there came a fear on all: and they glorified God, saying, That a great prophet is risen up among us; and, That God hath visited his people.* [17]*And this rumor of him went forth throughout all Judæa, and throughout all the region round about"* (Luke 7:11-17).

"[19]*For the earnest expectation of the creature waiteth for the manifestation of the sons of God"* (Romans 8:19).

I want you to know that you can stop these wicked powers and force them to bow through prayers. The woman with the issues of blood for twelve years stopped them and forced them to bow through the exercising of her faith in our Lord Jesus Christ. You too can rise up and begin to pray.

PRAYER POINTS

1. Any strongman that has vowed to ruin my life, be disgraced publicly, in the name of Jesus.
2. I convert all my past defeats to victories, in the name of Jesus.
3. I expose all my stubborn enemies to failures and disgrace by force, in the name of Jesus.
4. Every good ground I have lost to the devil, I reclaim you double, in the name of Jesus.
5. O Lord, arise and cause my stubborn enemies to bow and surrender, in the name of Jesus.
6. Let the judgment fire of God begin to burn my enemies until they bow, in the name of Jesus.
7. I weaken the powers of my enemies and I command them to bow, in the name of Jesus.
8. Every enemy of my destiny in the battlefield, receive defeat, in the name of Jesus.
9. Any sickness that has vowed to take me to the grave, I cast you out, in the name of Jesus.
10. Any evil arrow that has refused to leave me alone, come out by force, in the name of Jesus.
11. Any problem that has vowed to keep me in bondage forever, die, in the name of Jesus.
12. Let the Pharaohs of my destiny be disgrace to death, in the name of Jesus.
13. Any strange fire that is burning in my life, I quench you by force, in the name of Jesus.

14. Any unrepentant enemy that is militating against my life, I cut your head off, in the name of Jesus.

15. I break the backbone of my unrepentant enemies, in the name of Jesus.

16. Blood of Jesus, make life unbearable for sin and sickness in my life, in the name of Jesus.

17. Holy Ghost fire, burn every property of the devil in my life to ashes, in the name of Jesus.

18. Let every ancient problem in my life bow by force, in the name of Jesus.

19. Any evil leg that has walked into my life, walk out in shame, in the name of Jesus.

20. Any problem that entered into my life through my dreams, die, in the name of Jesus.

21. Any unrepentant witch or wizard that is trading with my destiny, be disgraced in the name of Jesus.

PRAYER TO MOVE GOD INTO ACTION

God's Word empowers Christians to move God into action. Many areas of our lives require God's attention and intervention. And this may not happen until we begin to pray according to God's Word and will.

> *"[9]Who will bring me into the strong city? Who will lead me into Edom?"* (Psalms 60:9).

> *"[1]Moreover the word of the LORD came unto Jeremiah the second time, while he was yet shut up in the court of the prison, saying, [2]Thus saith the LORD the maker thereof, the LORD that formed it, to establish it; the LORD is his name; [3]Call unto me, and I will answer thee, and shew thee great and mighty things, which thou knowest not"* (Jeremiah 33:1-3).

The devil has succeeded in building strongholds in many people's lives. Some demons are on suicide missions and are not ready to back down. It is only through prayer programs like this one can evil powers back down, surrender and leave. Usually, evil prophesies, hardship, problems, sickness and poverty have wicked demons attached to them. And when you don't resist such evil powers, they would never let you go.

> *"[7]Submit yourselves therefore to God. Resist the devil, and he will flee from you"* (James 4:7).

> *"[1]After this there was a feast of the Jews; and Jesus went up to Jerusalem. [2]Now there is at Jerusalem by the sheep market a pool, which is called in the Hebrew tongue Bethesda, having five porches. [3]In these lay a great multitude of impotent folk, of blind, halt, withered, waiting for the moving of the water.*

[4]*For an angel went down at a certain season into the pool, and troubled the water: whosoever then first after the troubling of the water stepped in was made whole of whatsoever disease he had.* [5]*And a certain man was there, which had an infirmity thirty and eight years.* [6]*When Jesus saw him lie, and knew that he had been now a long time in that case, he saith unto him, Wilt thou be made whole?* [7]*The impotent man answered him, Sir, I have no man, when the water is troubled, to put me into the pool: but while I am coming, another steppeth down before me.* [8]*Jesus saith unto him, Rise, take up thy bed, and walk.* [9]*And immediately the man was made whole, and took up his bed, and walked: and on the same day was the Sabbath"* (John 5:1-9).

Even through the bible, there were countless instances of difficult situations and problems that affected the people of God. For instance, Jacob ran away from his father's house because of problems. Joseph's brothers sold him, and he was imprisoned in Egypt. Barrenness conquered Hannah. Hunger and poverty threatened the life of the widow of Zarephath. Daniel was thrown into the den with lions. Esther, Mordecai and the tribes of Israel were marked for death. By the means of this program, God will rise and stop every evil movement going on in your life in the name of Jesus.

"[38]*Jesus therefore again groaning in himself cometh to the grave. It was a cave, and a stone lay upon it.* [39]*Jesus said, Take ye away the stone. Martha, the sister of him that was dead, saith unto him, Lord, by this time he stinketh: for he hath been dead four days.* [40]*Jesus saith unto her, Said I not unto thee, that, if thou wouldest believe, thou shouldest see the glory of God?* [41]*Then they took away the stone from the place where the dead was laid. And Jesus lifted up his eyes, and said, Father, I thank thee that thou hast heard me.* [42]*And I knew that thou hearest me always: but because of the people which stand by I said it, that they may believe that thou hast sent me.*

> [43]*And when he thus had spoken, he cried with a loud voice, Lazarus, come forth.* [44]*And he that was dead came forth, bound hand and foot with graveclothes: and his face was bound about with a napkin. Jesus saith unto them, Loose him, and let him go*" (John 11:38-44).

If God could stop Pharaoh, men of Sodom, Esau, Laban and Joseph's brethren, then He can as well stop your *Goliath*, disgrace your *Jezebel* and overthrow your *Bar Jesus*.

PRAYER POINTS

1. Any witch or wizard that is manipulating my life, become confused immediately, in the name of Jesus.

2. I command my life to move forward by force, in the name of Jesus.

3. Any man, woman or power that is sitting upon my blessings, be wasted, in the name of Jesus.

4. Fire of God, burn every enemy of my blessings to ashes, in the name of Jesus.

5. Let my life move God to act on my behalf by fire, in the name of Jesus.

6. I bring the presence of God everywhere I will go in life forever, in the name of Jesus.

7. Blood of Jesus, speak God into my life for a positive action, in the name of Jesus.

8. Let my life please God to enter into every city for deliverance, in the name of Jesus.

9. Blood of Jesus, empower me to make right choices in life, in the name of Jesus.

10. Every organized darkness that is enveloping my life, scatter and die, in the name of Jesus.

11. I break and loose myself from any form of demonic fear, in the name of Jesus.

12. Power to challenge any Goliath in every city, possess me, in the name of Jesus.

13. Let all giants in my Promised Land die by fire, in the name of Jesus.

14. Anointing to disgrace the devil and all his agents, posses me, in the name of Jesus.
15. O God, arise and restore me to Your perfect will, in the name of Jesus.
16. Any satanic padlock that is locking people in groups, I break you, in the name of Jesus.
17. I command every impossible thing in my life to bow at my command everywhere I go, in the name of Jesus.
18. I receive the key to open every door that is locked by the devil and his agents, in the name of Jesus.
19. I release every good thing that belongs to me in any nation, in the name of Jesus.
20. I move by the wind to destroy evil, in the name of Jesus.
21. I receive the mandate to bind and loose until devil bows, in the name of Jesus.

PRAYER TO OPEN CLOSED DOORS

Realities of opened or closed doors play out in so many people's lives every day. When doors are closed, people take wrong steps and make heinous mistakes. Sometimes, such mistakes cost their lives or livelihood.

At one point, Abraham went to Egypt to beg for bread because of famine.

> *"[10]And there was a famine in the land: and Abram went down into Egypt to sojourn there; for the famine was grievous in the land. [11]And it came to pass, when he was come near to enter into Egypt, that he said unto Sarai his wife, Behold now, I know that thou art a fair woman to look upon: [12]Therefore it shall come to pass, when the Egyptians shall see thee, that they shall say, This is his wife: and they will kill me, but they will save thee alive. [13]Say, I pray thee, thou art my sister: that it may be well with me for thy sake; and my soul shall live because of thee. [14]And it came to pass, that, when Abram was come into Egypt, the Egyptians beheld the woman that she was very fair. [15]The princes also of Pharaoh saw her, and commended her before Pharaoh: and the woman was taken into Pharaoh's house. [16]And he entreated Abram well for her sake: and he had sheep, and oxen, and he asses, and menservants, and maidservants, and she asses, and camels. [17]And the LORD plagued Pharaoh and his house with great plagues because of Sarai Abram's wife. [18]And Pharaoh called Abram, and said, What is this that thou hast done unto me? why didst thou not tell me that she was thy wife?"* (Genesis 12:10-18).

Close doors are common in every generation. When the doors of Sodom and Gomorrah were closed against Lot's wife, she looked behind and turned into a pillar of salt. Her two daughters, who escaped with Lot, committed incest with their father. Esau sold his birthright. Achan coveted Babylon's garments and died by being stoned together with his entire household. Saul sought for the help of a witch at the end of his life. And Ahithophel committed suicide.

> "[9]*For a great door and effectual is opened unto me, and there are many adversaries*" (1 Corinthians 16:9).

> "[1]*Now Jericho was straitly shut up because of the children of Israel: none went out, and none came in*" (Joshua 6:1).

> "[18]*Wherefore we would have come unto you, even I Paul, once and again; but Satan hindered us*" (1 Thessalonians 2:18).

A close door experience is an experience that often occurs in people's lives. God opened a great door for Paul, but the devil used fierce opposing to close it. Many adversaries rose up against his evangelistic ministry. Sometimes, you need to force your closed doors open, otherwise they would remain closed. These prayers will help you greatly as pray to open all your spiritual doors of blessings, as God moves to open all your closed doors.

> "[6]*This is the generation of them that seek him, that seek thy face, O Jacob. Selah.* [7]*Lift up your heads, O ye gates; and be ye lift up, ye everlasting doors; and the King of glory shall come in.* [8]*Who is this King of glory? The LORD strong and mighty, the LORD mighty in battle*" (Psalms 24:6-8).

I pray that every satanic limitation must be overcome as you go through this program with all seriousness and hope.

PRAYER POINTS

1. I command every good door that was closed against my life to open by force, in the name of Jesus.
2. Any evil personality that is blocking my way, be removed by force, in the name of Jesus.
3. You, the strongman of my place of birth that is attacking my destiny, die, in the name of Jesus.
4. I command the Red Sea to divide again by force, in the name of Jesus.
5. You, walls of Jericho that is blocking my way, collapse by thunder, in the name of Jesus.
6. Any satanic padlock that is locking up my finance, break to pieces, in the name of Jesus.
7. O Lord, arise and take me over to the other side of blessings, in the name of Jesus.
8. Let my doors for unspeakable greatness open by force, in the name of Jesus.
9. Father Lord, help me to operate in an open door, in the name of Jesus.
10. Every evil limitation in my life, disappear by force, in the name of Jesus.
11. Blood of Jesus, open every good door my enemies have closed against my life, in the name of Jesus.
12. Every door that will lead me to my divine resources, open for me, in the name of Jesus.
13. Any problem in my life that has closed good doors against me, die, in the name of Jesus.

14. Blood of Jesus, speak every closed door against me to open, in the name of Jesus.

15. Any sin in my life that has closed my heavens, die, in the name of Jesus.

16. Any satanic army that is standing at the doors of my destiny, die, in the name of Jesus.

17. Any problem that is designed to stop my journey, be destroyed, in the name of Jesus.

18. Father Lord, open the doors of miracles for my life, in the name of Jesus.

19. I command every satanic gate that is constructed against me to break, in the name of Jesus.

20. O Lord, arise and lead me to the doors of my blessings, in the name of Jesus.

21. Any ancient door that is closed against my life, open by force, in the name of Jesus.

PRAYER TO RELEASE YOUR BURDENS

Many people live their everyday lives under unbearable burdens. There is no need to carry burdens from place to place when Jesus has promised to give you rest. Why must you then die under an unbearable burden?

> "[28]*Come unto me, all ye that labor and are heavy laden, and I will give you rest.* [29]*Take my yoke upon you, and learn of me; for I am meek and lowly in heart: and ye shall find rest unto your souls.* [30]*For my yoke is easy, and my burden is light*" (Matthew 11:28-30).

For many years, Hannah had a problem of conception. It was a case of reproach, shame and disgrace. But she went to God and He took away her burden. Sickness, diseases and infirmities are burdens, which you must take to God through prayers.

> "[7]*Ask, and it shall be given you; seek, and ye shall find; knock, and it shall be opened unto you:* [8]*For every one that asketh receiveth; and he that seeketh findeth; and to him that knocketh it shall be opened.* [9]*Or what man is there of you, whom if his son ask bread, will he give him a stone?* [10]*Or if he ask a fish, will he give him a serpent?* [11]*If ye then, being evil, know how to give good gifts unto your children, how much more shall your Father which is in heaven give good things to them that ask him?*" (Matthew 7:7-11).

Equally, many people are suffering from poverty, untimely deaths, marital failures, late marriages and financial difficulties. You cannot afford to carry these burdens upon your shoulder any longer. Take them to God in prayers today and you will be free.

PRAYER POINTS

1. Owners of evil load in my life, appear and carry your loads, in the name of Jesus.
2. I cut off anything in my life that is hindering the move of the Spirit, in the name of Jesus.
3. Father Lord, inject in me Your power to release my burdens, in the name of Jesus.
4. I receive divine help to live above problems and challenges, in the name of Jesus.
5. I command my life to be rooted and grounded in prosperity from God, in the name of Jesus.
6. O Lord, remove every demonic deposit in my life, in the name of Jesus.
7. Every evil utterance in my life that is assigned to torment me to death, die, in the name of Jesus.
8. I receive the anointing to overcome every problem, in the name of Jesus.
9. Father Lord, feed me with the food of the winners, in the name of Jesus.
10. I cut myself off from family inherited burdens, in the name of Jesus.
11. I break and loose myself from burdens of environments, in the name of Jesus.
12. Blood of Jesus, flow into my life and speak for my freedom from evil burdens, in the name of Jesus.
13. Every burden in my life that is causing me to be ridiculed, drop by force, in the name of Jesus.

14. Any demonic stronghold that is promoting my burdens, collapse, in the name of Jesus.

15. Any power that is sponsoring my burdens, be exposed and be destroyed, in the name of Jesus.

16. Let any stubborn strongman that has placed evil yoke on my head break it and die, in the name of Jesus.

17. Every enemy of my peace and rest, die, in the name of Jesus.

18. I command the yoke of my Goliath to break, in the name of Jesus.

19. Every spirit of Herod that is tormenting my life, come out and die, in the name of Jesus.

20. Any evil personality that is pursuing me with burdens, die, in the name of Jesus.

21. I cut myself off from demonic burdens, in the name of Jesus.

22. I command every demonic poison in my life to fade away, in the name of Jesus.

23. Any area of my life that has been arrested by evil forces, be released, in the name Jesus.

24. I command ancestral yokes in my life to break, in the name of Jesus.

25. Let satanic bondages that have vowed to follow me to the grave break, in the name of Jesus.

26. Let the burdens of poverty in my life break to pieces, in the name of Jesus.

27. Let witchcraft burdens in my life drop by force, in the name of Jesus.

28. Every demonic agent that is assigned to keep me in bondage, be frustrated, in the name of Jesus.

29. Let all Delilah and Jezebels in my life be disgraced, in the name of Jesus.

30. I break and deliver myself from any addiction, in the name of Jesus.

31. Any spell that is cast upon my life, loose your hold by force, in the name of Jesus.

32. I chase away every evil spirit that is promoting my burdens, in the name of Jesus.

33. Every evil door that is opened for evil spirits to enter my life, close, in the name of Jesus.

34. Father Lord, empower me with Your kingdom lifestyle, in the name of Jesus.

35. O Lord, create a wall of fire between evil burdens and I, in the name of Jesus.

36. You, demons that are energizing all kinds of burden in my life, I cast you out, in the name of Jesus.

PRAYER TO WIN IN COMPETITIONS

People, who labor to win in all competitions, are always ready to keep the rules and obey God. But when you shortchange God in order to win, you set yourself up for greater loss at last. Pray for the spirit of excellence and trust God in all things you do.

> *"[1]It pleased Darius to set over the kingdom an hundred and twenty princes, which should be over the whole kingdom; [2]And over these three presidents; of whom Daniel was first: that the princes might give accounts unto them, and the king should have no damage. [3]Then this Daniel was preferred above the presidents and princes, because an excellent spirit was in him; and the king thought to set him over the whole realm"* (Daniel 6:1-3).

> *"[13]And the LORD shall make thee the head, and not the tail; and thou shalt be above only, and thou shalt not be beneath; if that thou hearken unto the commandments of the LORD thy God, which I command thee this day, to observe and to do them"* (Deuteronomy 28:13).

When you prayerfully do what is expected of you, the Lord helps you to excel. God is able to make your performances to be exceptional and you will perform above the rest. God desires that His children excel in this world for the sake of His kingdom. If you wish to be preferred above others and become outstanding, then you must fight to rise to the top by doing all that God and authorities expect of you.

PRAYER POINTS

1. O Lord, make me a better competitor, in the name of Jesus.
2. Let my star rise and shine brightly in this competition, in the name of Jesus.
3. O Lord, upgrade my destiny, in the name of Jesus.
4. Power to be preferred above others, possess me now, in the name of Jesus.
5. Blood of Jesus, beautify me to Your glory, in the name of Jesus.
6. Every enemy of my destination, die by force, in the name of Jesus.
7. O Lord, put me ahead of others, in the name of Jesus.
8. Any evil personality that is pushing me behind, die by force, in the name of Jesus.
9. O Lord, let me find favor from the decision makers, in the name of Jesus.
10. Lord Jesus, walk me up to the top, in the name of Jesus.
11. I receive the power to become a standard, in the name of Jesus.
12. O Lord, influence the panel of judges to give me the highest mark, in the name of Jesus.
13. Any evil mark upon my life, disappear, in the name of Jesus.
14. Any spirit of fear and failure in my life, die by force, in the name of Jesus.
15. Anything in my life that is pulling me backward, die, in the name of Jesus.

16. Any covenant or curse of backwardness, expire now, in the name of Jesus.

17. Any evil mobility that is pushing me to the back seat, be demobilized, in the name of Jesus

18. O Lord, arise and feed me with the food of the champions, in the name of Jesus.

19. Let my appearance be like that of an angel of God, in the name of Jesus.

20. O Lord, make me the prime star and a celebrity in my generation, in the name of Jesus.

21. I reject every arrow of disappointment, in the name of Jesus.

22. I reject failure and defeat from my life forever, in the name of Jesus.

23. Any wall of Jericho that is standing against my efforts, collapse, in the name of Jesus.

24. O Lord, bless me exceedingly to triumph highly for Your glory, in the name Jesus.

Other titles in this series – ALONE WITH GOD

1. **Prayers for Good Health**

Prayers in this series include prayers to overcome asthma, diabetes, high blood pressure, surgeries, cancer, brain tumor, ectopic and prolong pregnancies, facial disease, fibroid and evil plantations, heart enlargement, incurable diseases, insanity, mental illness, sleeplessness, ulcers, heart disease, safe delivery, strokes, kidney problem, pneumonia, fever, poison, demonic burns, dog bite poisons, diarrhea, epilepsy, toothache and breast lump.

2. **Prayers for Financial Breakthrough**

Prayers in this series include prayers for financial assistance, finance breakthrough, financial miracles, divine breakthrough and opportunities, divine connections, business breakthrough, divine promotion, prosperity, protection from enemies, protection from evil, deliverance from poverty, overcoming enemies in the place of work, paying bills, prospering in business, divine connections, prospering in foreign land, recovering lost businesses, recovering a lost job, recovering all your loss, reviving collapsed or collapsing business, revoking evil decrees, rise from defeat, searching and finding jobs, stopping determined enemies, succeeding where others are failing and prayers to survive economic meltdown/famine.

3. **Prayers for Marriage & Family**

Prayers in this series deal with attacks at home, polygamous spirit, eating and having sex in dreams, having sex outside marriage, sexual weaknesses among legally married couples, broken homes, husbands who experience hatred from their wives, people who become sexually active with outsiders only, people who become sexually weak before their spouse, families in distress, men who are captured by strange women, true friendship, a godly woman, men who are sexually disconnected from their wives, women who experience hatred from their husbands, women who trust God for a child at old age, bear godly children, end a spirit marriage, become fertile and productive, deliver your children, frustrate divorce plans, keep your pregnancy, prevent miscarriage, end prolonged pregnancy, end separation plans, stop the enemies of your marriage and prayers to overcome troubles in your marriage.

4. **Prayers against Satanic Oppression**

Prayers in this series include prayers for protection from evil spirits, overcoming hopelessness, against all odds, arrows in the dream, attacks on churches, bewitchment, the spirit of confusion, marine curses, marine covenants, natural disasters, opposition at the work place, destroyers of environments, attacks in the dream, graveyard spirits, the power of sin, unknown enemies, overturn your defeats, disengage evil partners, overcome stress, crush witchcraft attacks, cross over to the next level, close witchcraft doors, cast out sexual demons, cast out demon of epilepsy and prayers to burn satanic liabilities.

5. **Prayers for Children & Youth**

Prayers in this series include prayers for bachelors and spinsters, before birthday, 3 days prayer for school children, children whose parents are divorced, victory at all cost, young school children, youths and teenagers, train children well.

6. **Prayers for Overcoming Attitude Problems**

Prayers in this series include prayers to overcome drug addiction, avoid criminal records, outlive death threats, overcome destructive habits, overcome fearful and intimidating problems, frustrations, deal with kidnappers and prayers to overcome evil habits.

7. **Prayers for Academic Success**

Prayers in this section include prayers for success in examination, prayers before examination, during examination, after examination, prayers for breakthrough in examination, prayers before an interview and prayer for undergraduates.

8. **Prayers for A Successful Career**

Prayers in this series include prayers to keep your job and destiny, for footballers, career people, for great and immediate changes, for guidance, new job, for sportsmen and women, best employment, to be self or gainfully employed, for a better job, enter into a new place, excel above your masters, excel in a job interview, force your enemies out of comfort, force your enemies to bow, move God into action, open closed doors, unburden your burdens and prayer to win in competitions.

9. **Prayers for Deliverance**

Prayers in this series include prayers for deliverance, against evil marks, evil traditions, for family tree, break the seal of bondage, break the yoke of death, destroy evil delays, destroy evil movements in the body, destroy serpents in the body, against your sinful pasts, for peace of mind, total freedom, stop the wicked, stop future enemies

10. **Special Prayers in His Presence**

Prayers in this series include prayers to win court, hospital and police cases, prayer at new year eves, for Africa, blessings, citizenship, cleansing, comfort, compassion, confidence, courage, Good Friday, Easter Sunday morning, Easter Saturday, encouragement, journey mercies, fellowship, ministry, to be touched for Christ, for residence permits, right decisions, safety, security, sponsorship, United Nations, Valentine's day, to be selected among the eleven, to preserve America and prayers to overcome all unknown problems.

11. Alone With God (Complete version) – This is the complete version of the ten-part series of ALONE WITH GOD. This book can be a highly resourceful prayer companion in your libraries and prayer ministries.

Thank You So Much!

Beloved, I hope you enjoyed this book as much as I believe God has touched your heart today. I cannot thank you enough for your continued support for this prayer ministry.

I appreciate you so much for taking out time to read this wonderful prayer book, and if you have an extra second, I would love to hear what you think about this book.

Please, do share your testimonies with me by sending an email to me at pastor@prayermadueke.com, or in Facebook at www.facebook.com/prayer.madueke. I personally invite you also to my website at www.prayermadueke.com to view many other books I have written on various issues of life, especially on marriage, family, sexual problems and money.

I will be delighted to partner with you in organized crusades, ceremonies, marriages and Marriage seminars, special events, church ministration and fellowship for the advancement of God's Kingdom here on earth.

Thank you again, and I wish you nothing less than success in life.

God bless you.

Prayer M. Madueke

OTHER BOOKS BY PRAYER M. MADUEKE

- *21/40 Nights Of Decrees And Your Enemies Will Surrender*
- *Confront And Conquer*
- *Tears in Prison*
- *35 Special Dangerous Decrees*
- *The Reality of Spirit Marriage*
- *Queen of Heaven*
- *Leviathan the Beast*
- *100 Days Prayer To Wake Up Your Lazarus*
- *Dangerous Decrees To Destroy Your Destroyers*
- *The spirit of Christmas*
- *More Kingdoms To Conquer*
- *Your Dream Directory*
- *The Sword Of New Testament Deliverance*
- *Alphabetic Battle For Unmerited Favors*
- *Alphabetic Character Deliverance*
- *Holiness*
- *The Witchcraft Of The Woman That Sits Upon Many Waters*
- *The Operations Of The Woman That Sits Upon Many Waters*
- *Powers To Pray Once And Receive Answers*
- *Prayer Riots To Overthrow Divorce*
- *Prayers To Get Married Happily*
- *Prayers To Keep Your Marriage Out of Troubles*
- *Prayers For Conception And Power To Retain*
- *Prayer Retreat – Prayers to Possess Your Year*
- *Prayers for Nation Building (Volumes 1, 2 & 3)*
- *Organized student in a disorganized school*
- *Welcome to Campus*
- *Alone with God (10 series)*

CONTACTS

AFRICA

#1 Babatunde close,
Off Olaitan Street, Surulere
Lagos, Nigeria
+234 803 353 0599
pastor@prayermadueke.com,

#28B Ubiaja Crescent
Garki II Abuja,
FCT - Nigeria
+234 807 065 4159

IRELAND

Ps Emmanuel Oko
#84 Thornfield Square
Cloudalkin D22
Ireland
Tel: +353 872 820 909, +353 872 977 422
aghaoko2003@yahoo.com

EUROPE/SCHENGEN

Collins Kwame
#46 Felton Road
Barking
Essex IG11 7XZ GB
Tel: +44 208 507 8083, +44 787 703 2386, +44 780 703 6916
aghaoko2003@yahoo.com

Made in the USA
Middletown, DE
04 October 2022